MOUNTS
Coloring book

AUTHOR AND ILLUSTRATOR
OLGA GOLOVESHKINA

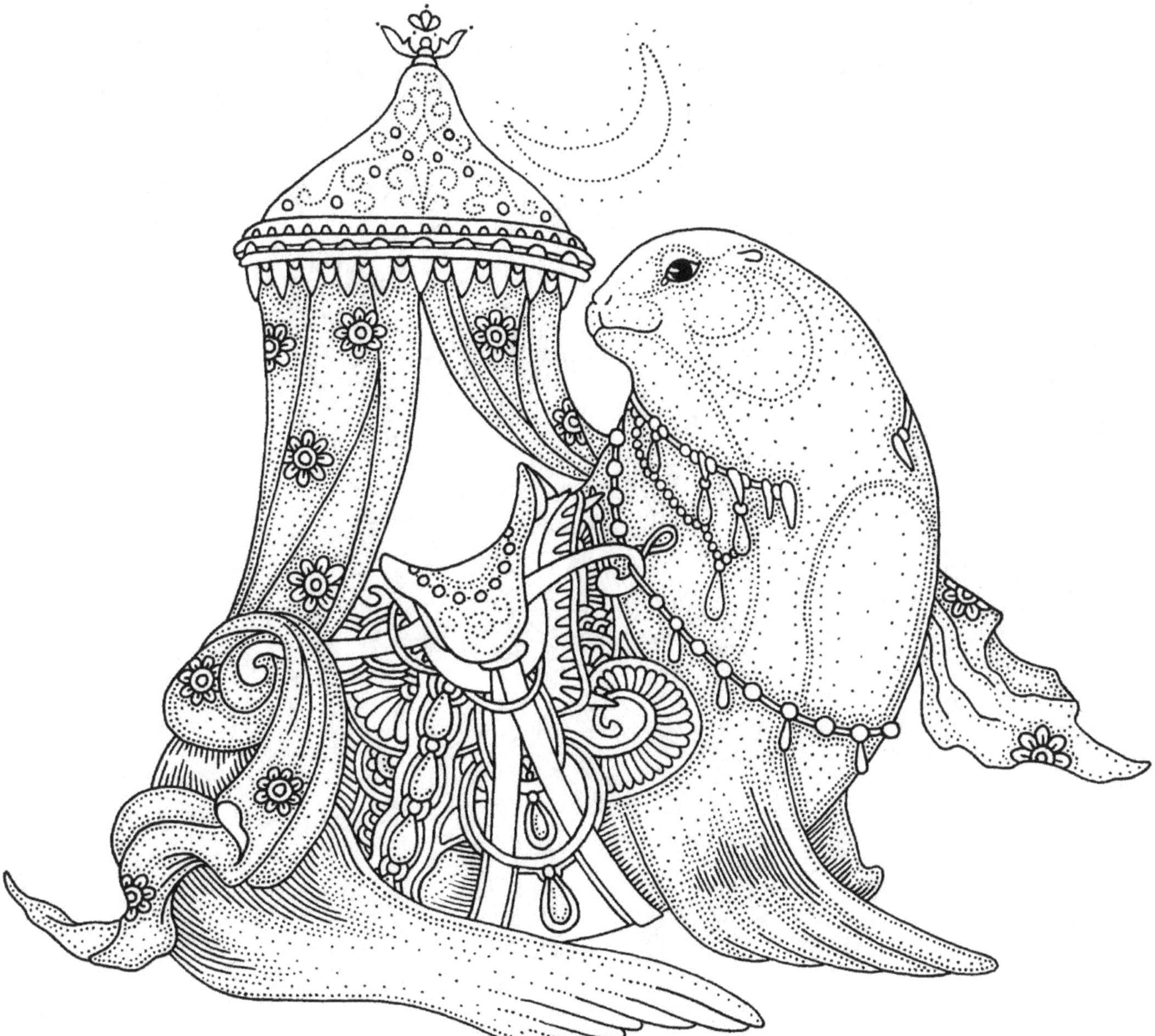

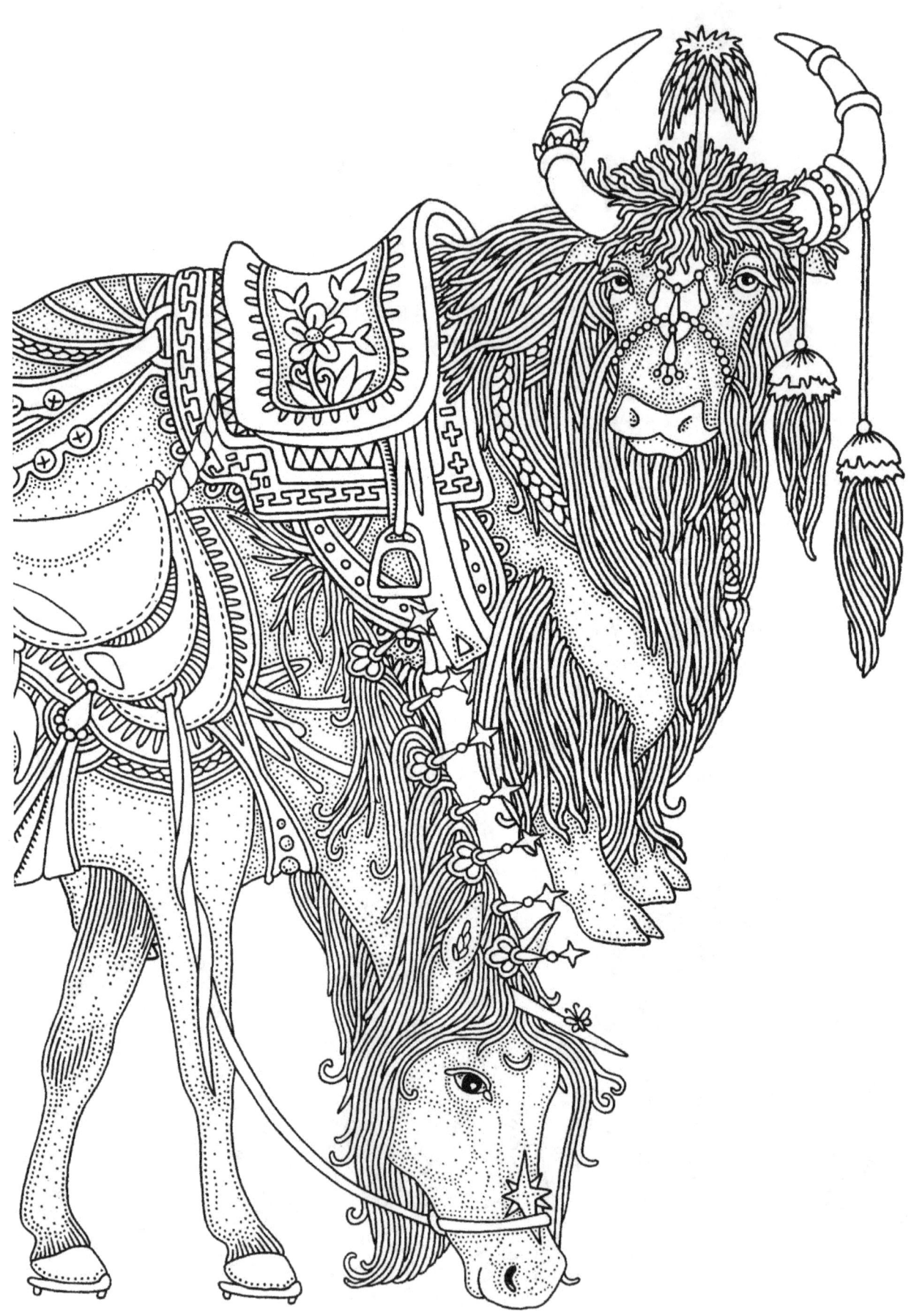

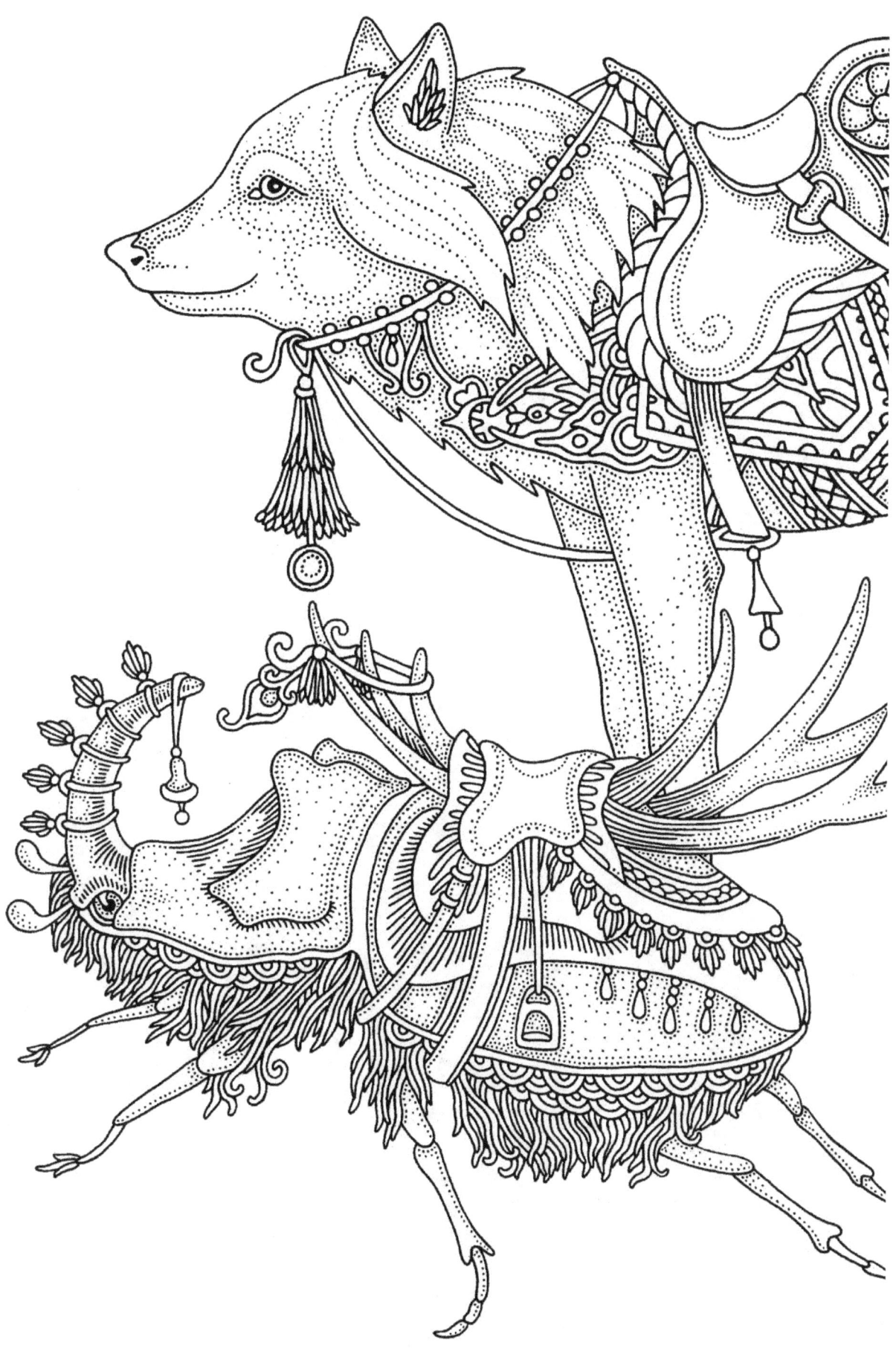

ISBN:1535247614
ISBN-13:9781535247610

Happy coloring

Thank you for choosing
my coloring book!

Olya :)

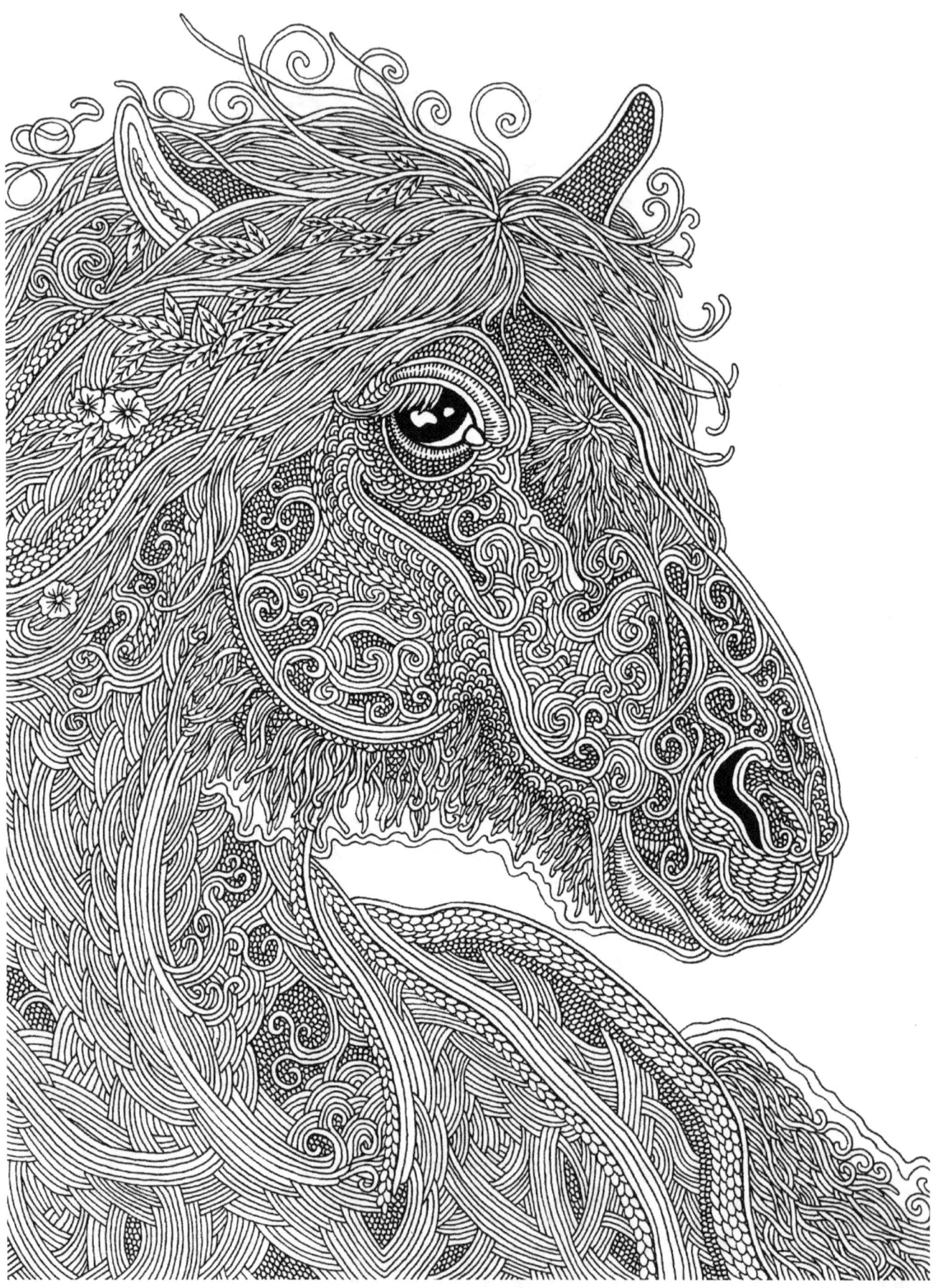

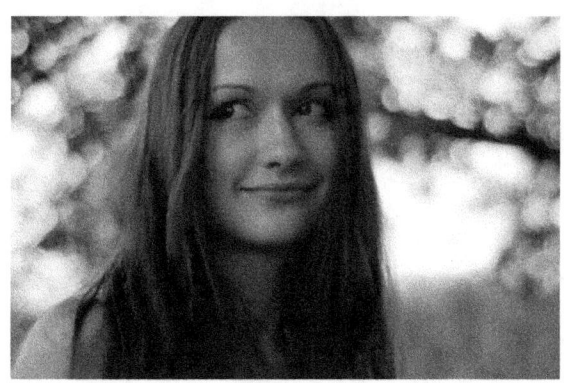

ABOUT THE AUTHOR

Olga Goloveshkina is a freelance artist and illustrator based in Moscow, Russia. She graduated from the Institute of Busines and Design. Olga specializes in black ink doodles.

She is an author and illustrator coloring books for adults "The wind carries flowers"/"Veter unosit tsvety" (in Russian), "Fox travel: Coloring book" and "Mounts: Coloring book" (in English).

Author page on Amazon:

amazon.com/author/olgagoloveshkina

Site:

http://olyagoloveshkina.jimdo.com

Instagram:

@olyahitrayapanda

@olyagoloveshkina

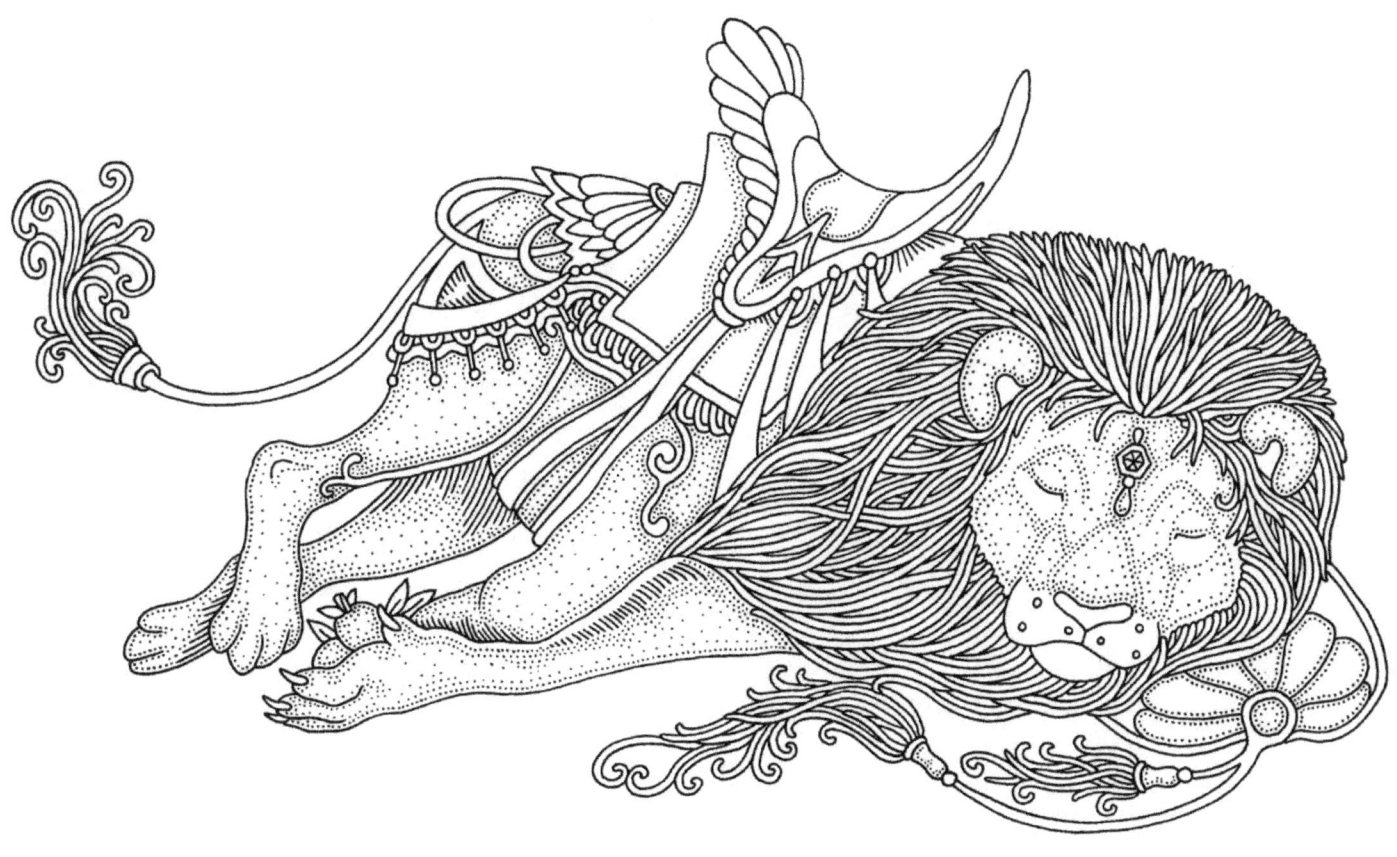

This book belongs to

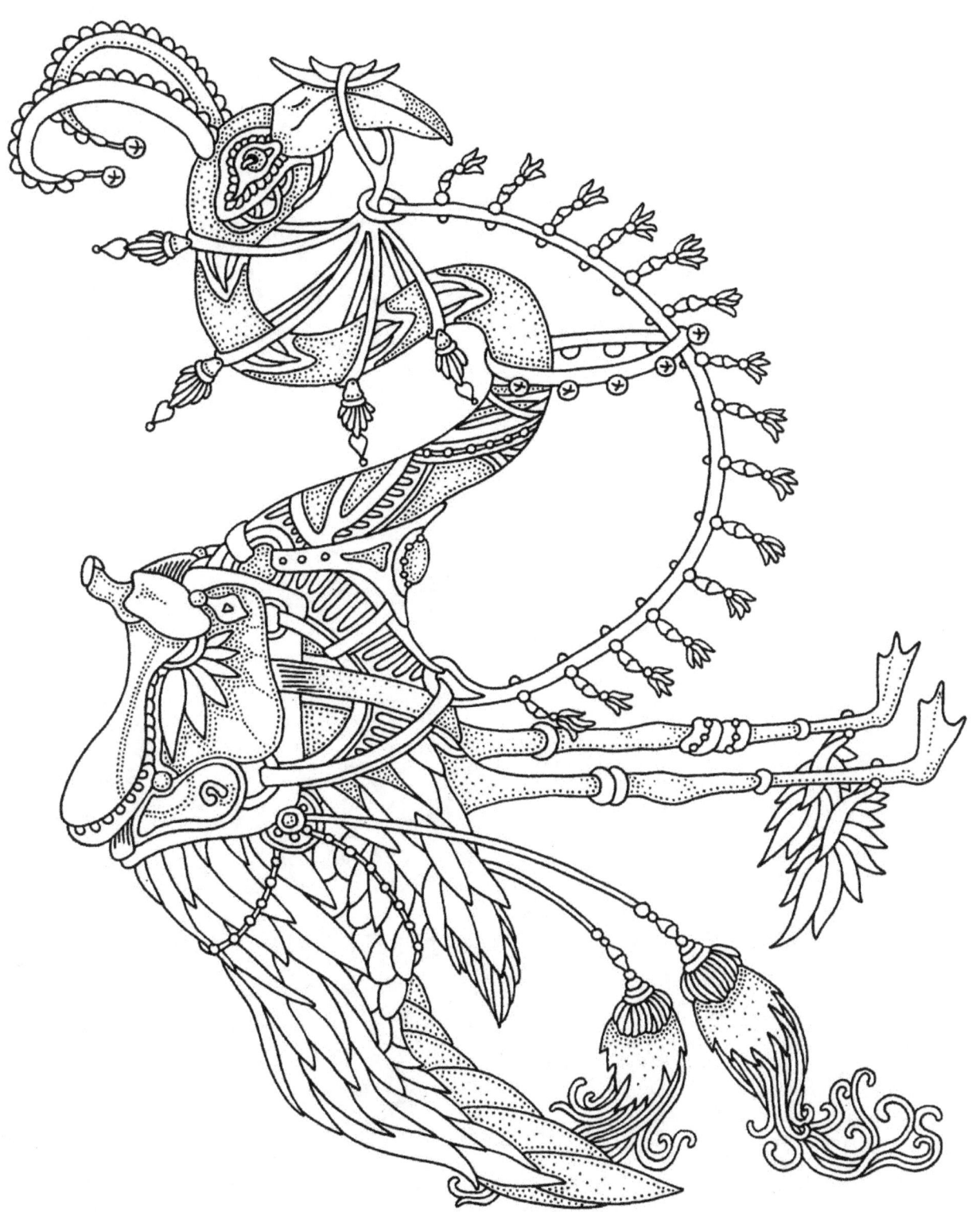

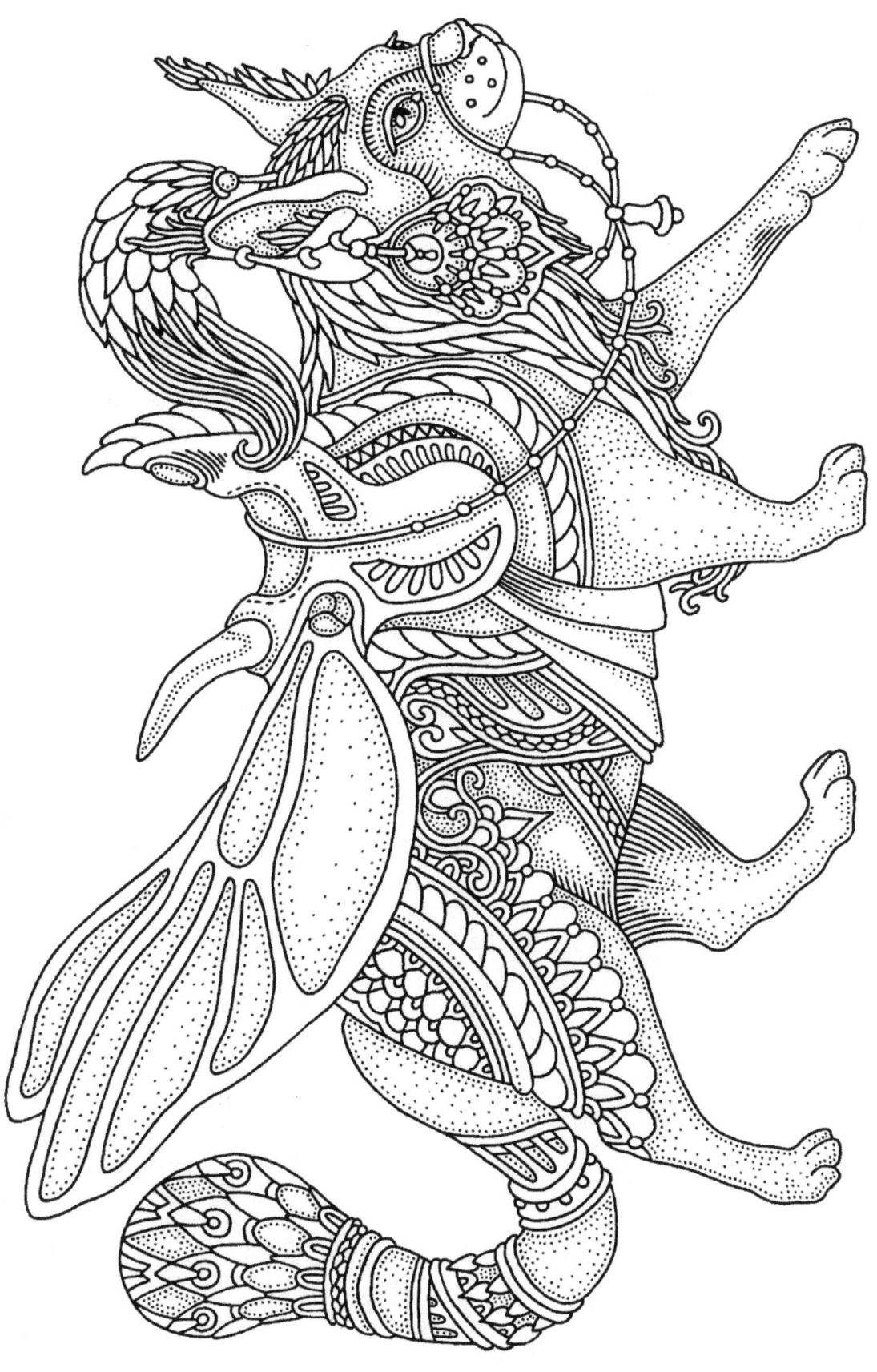

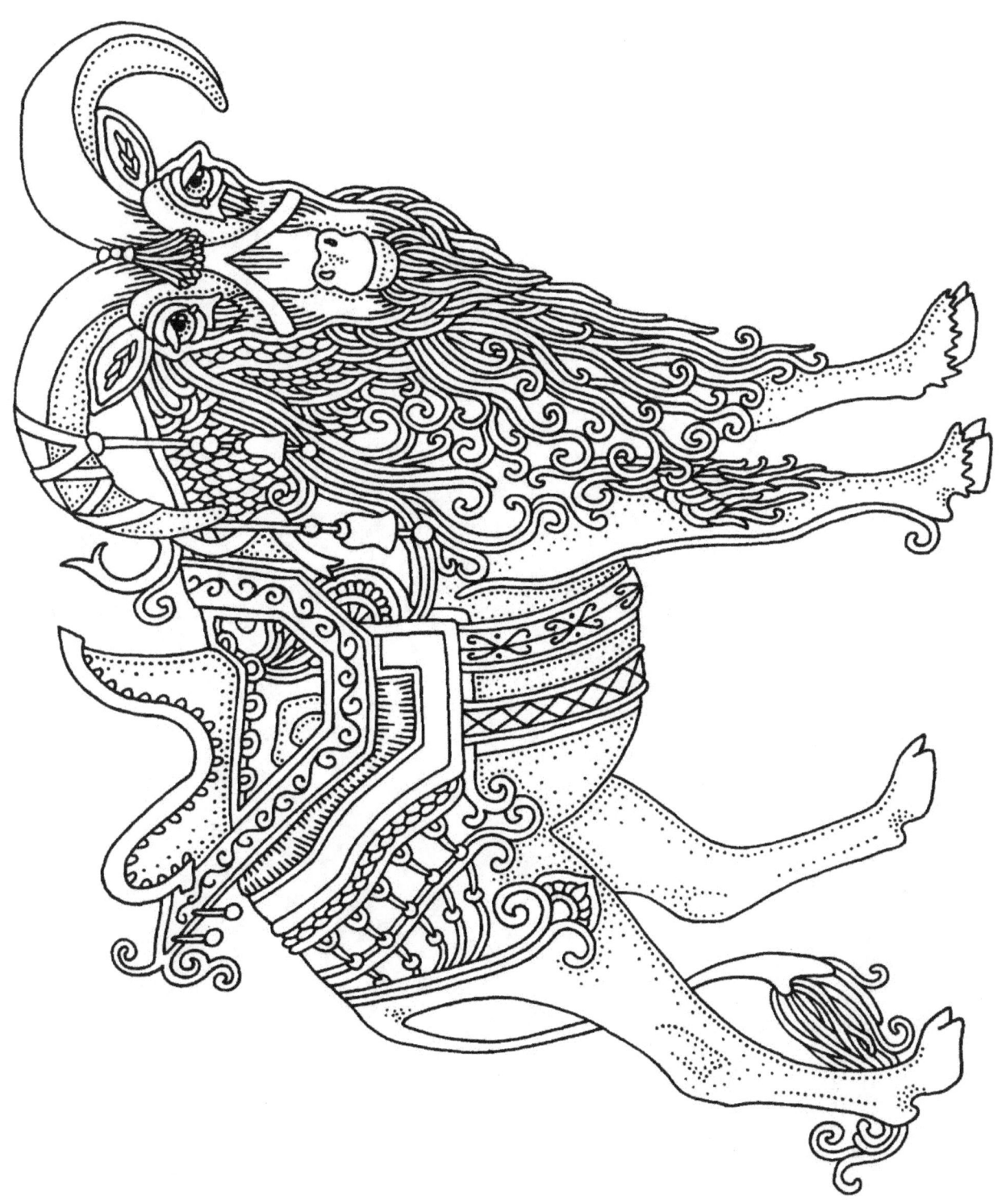

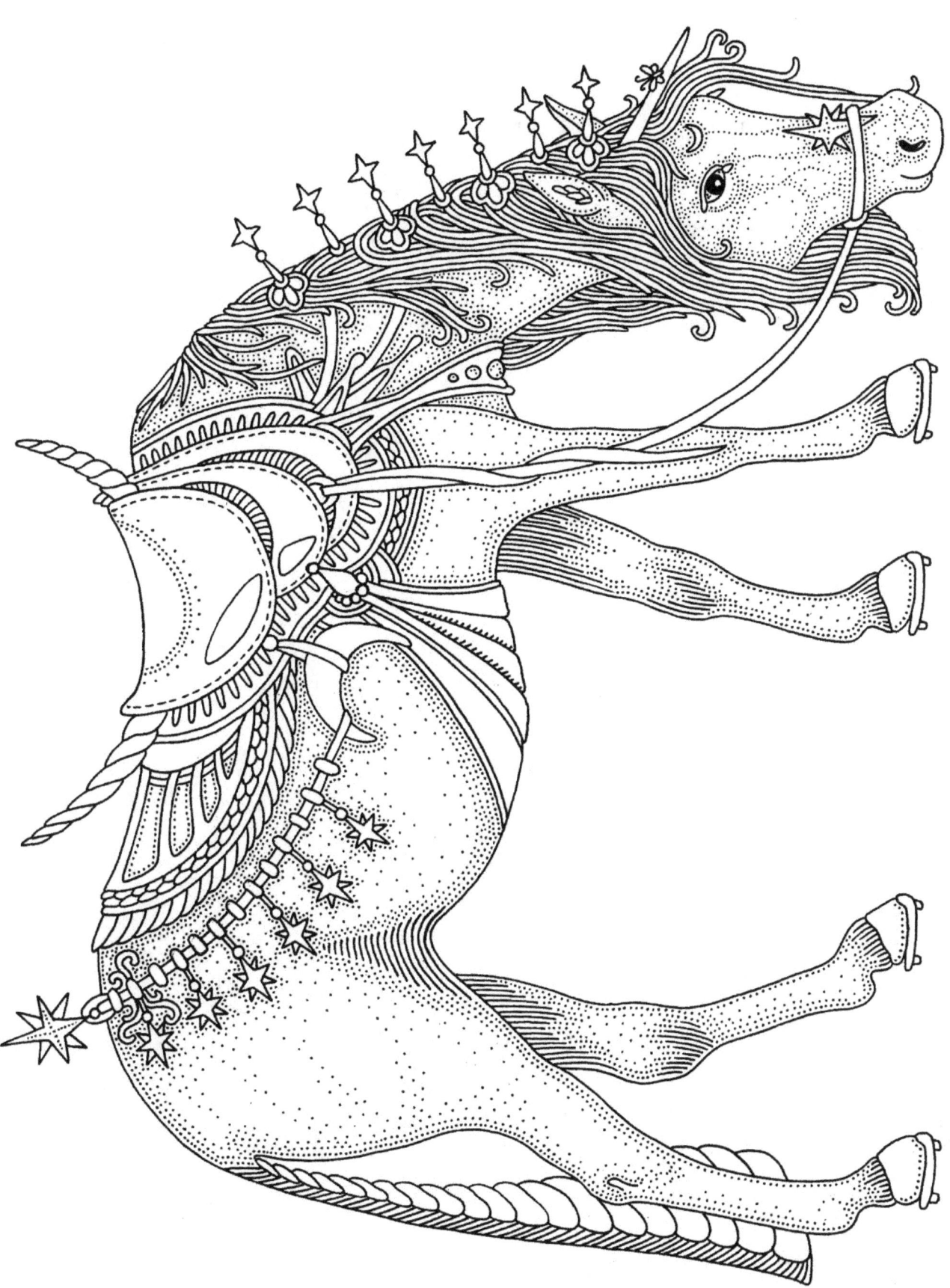

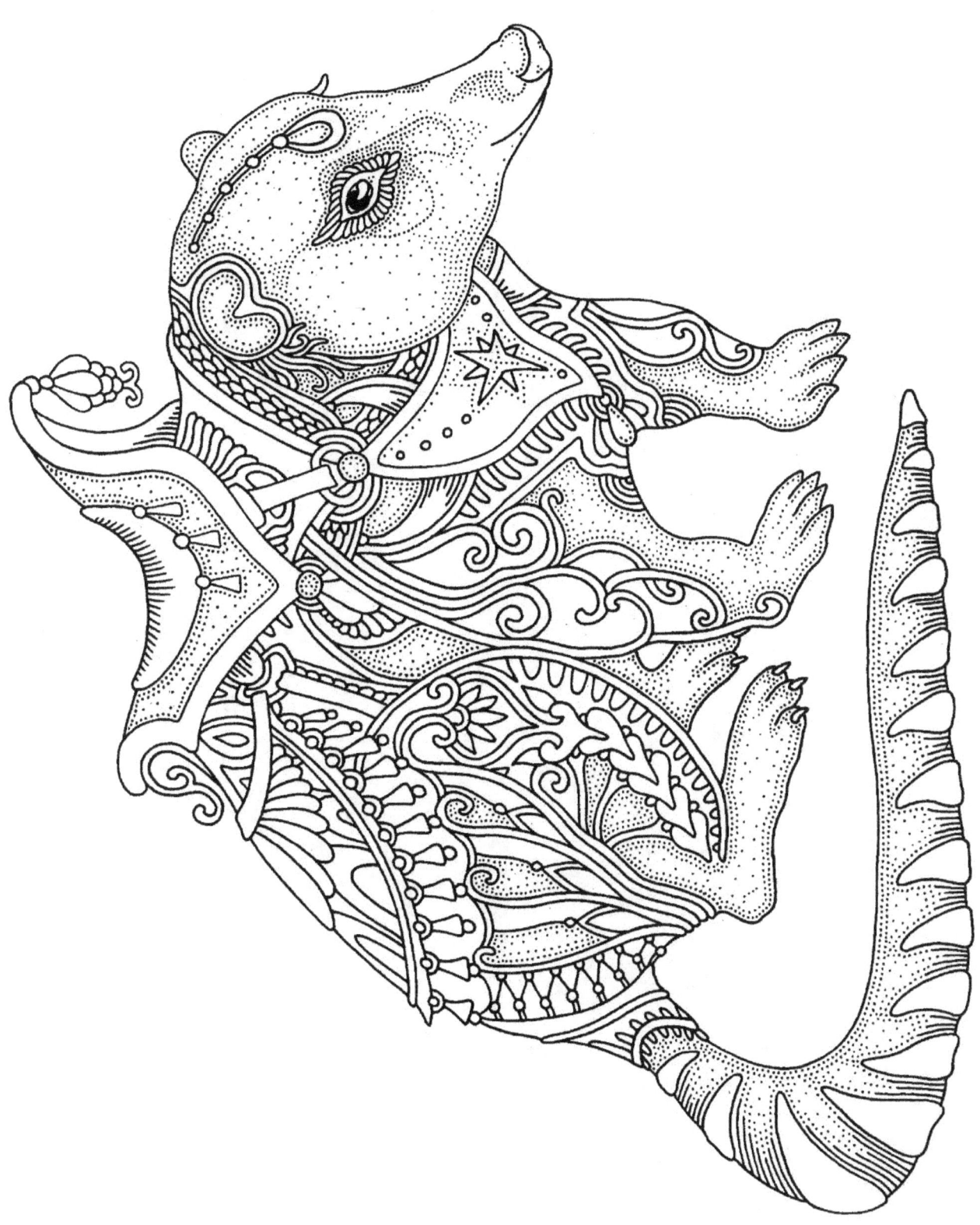

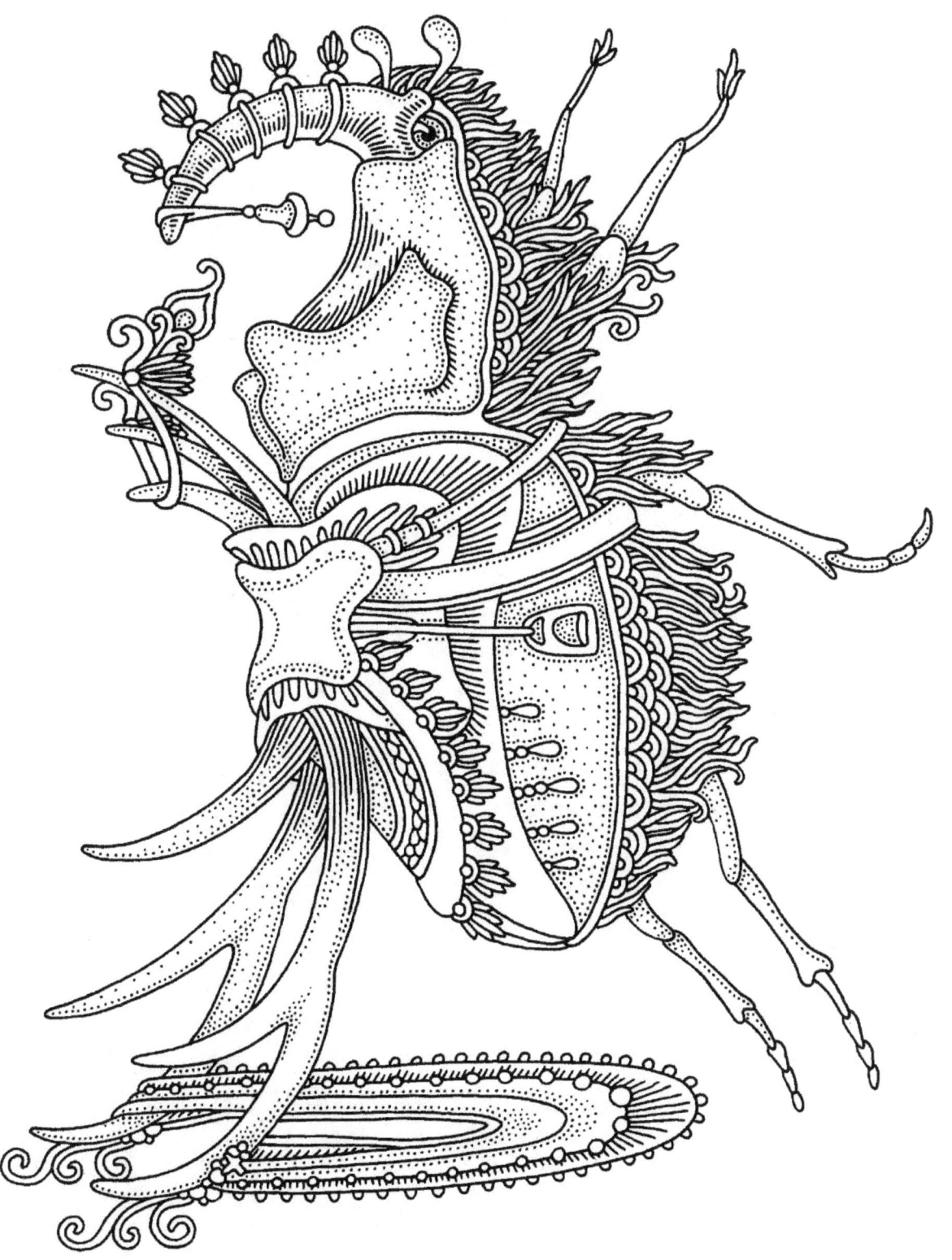

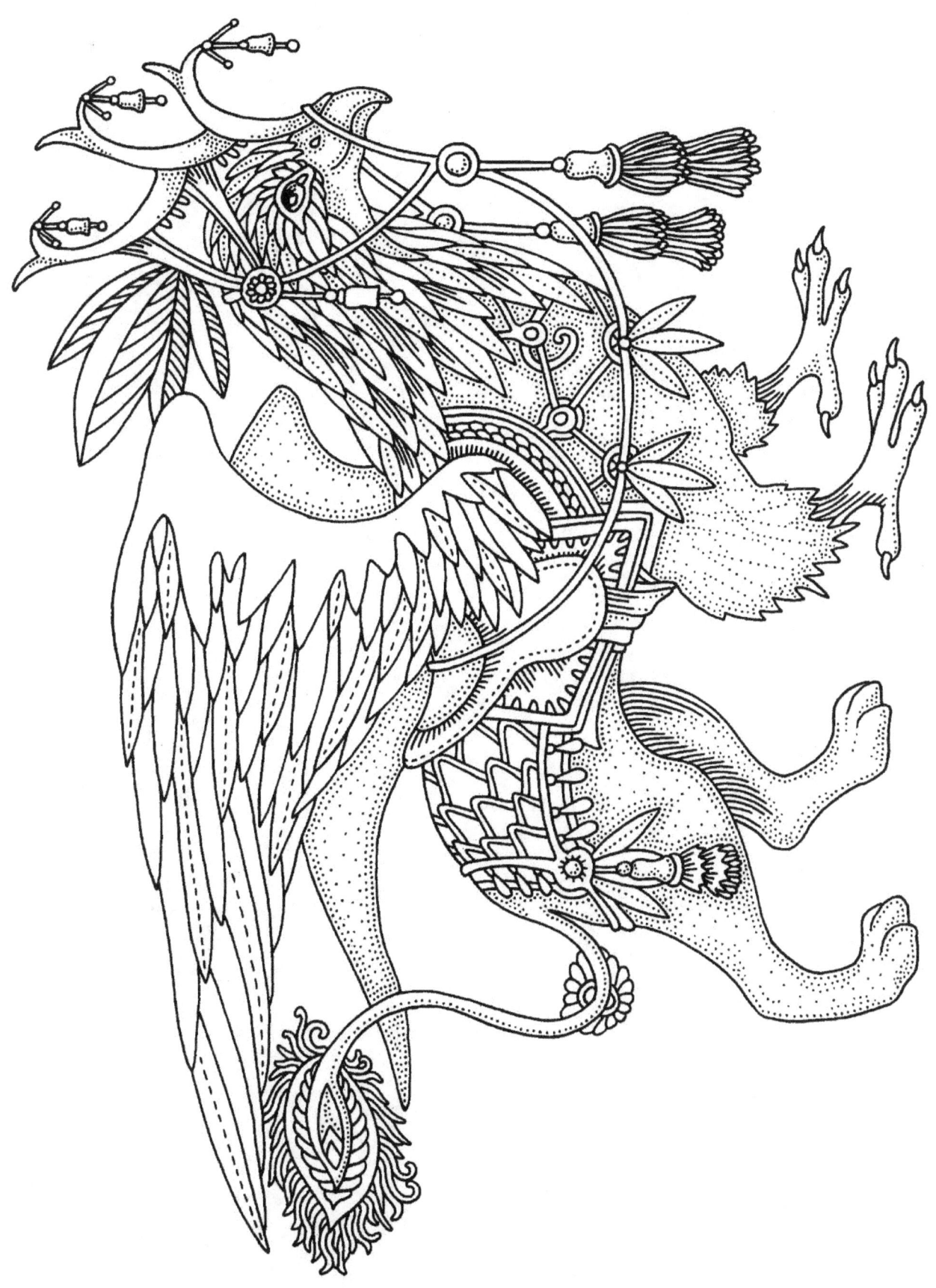

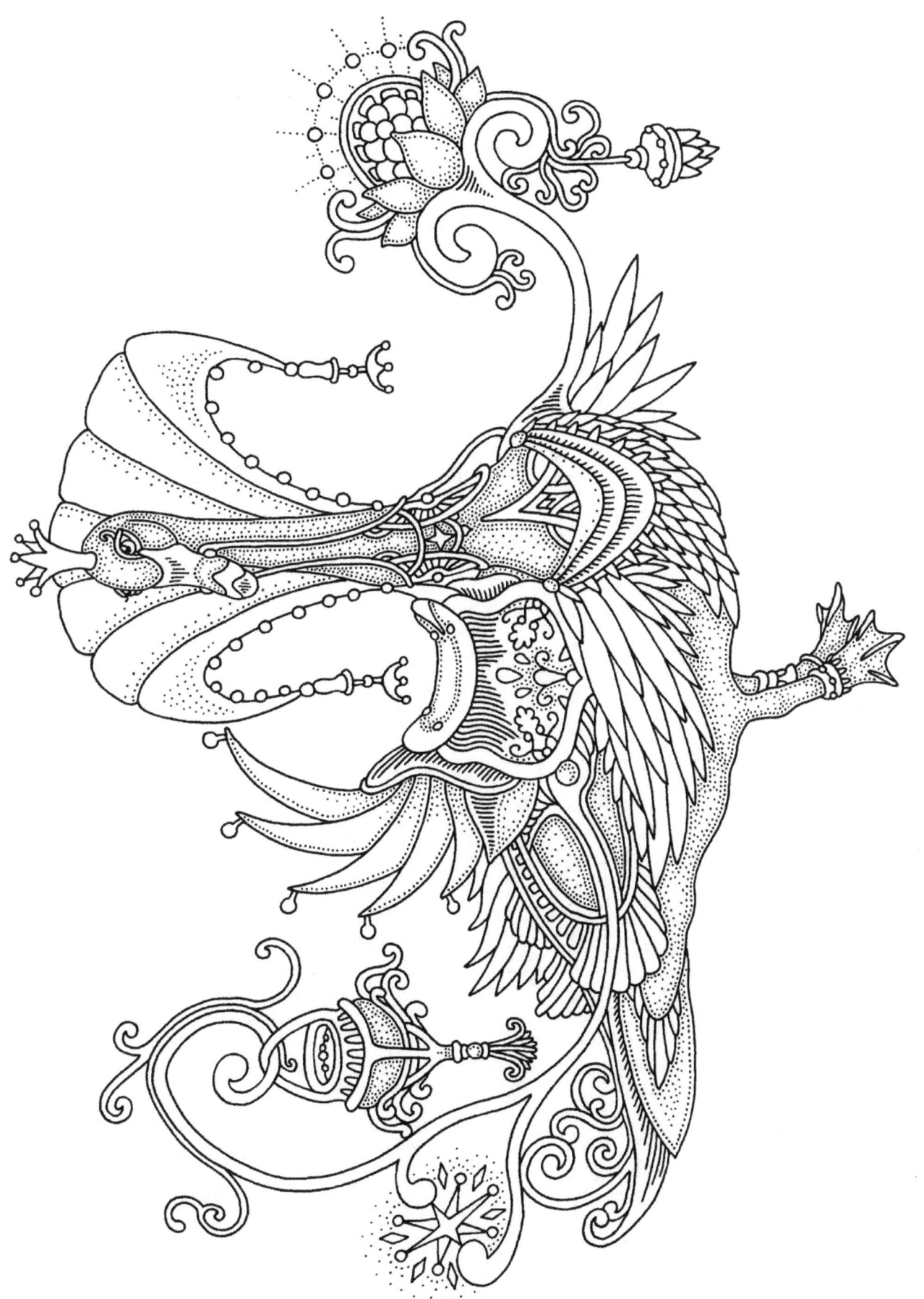

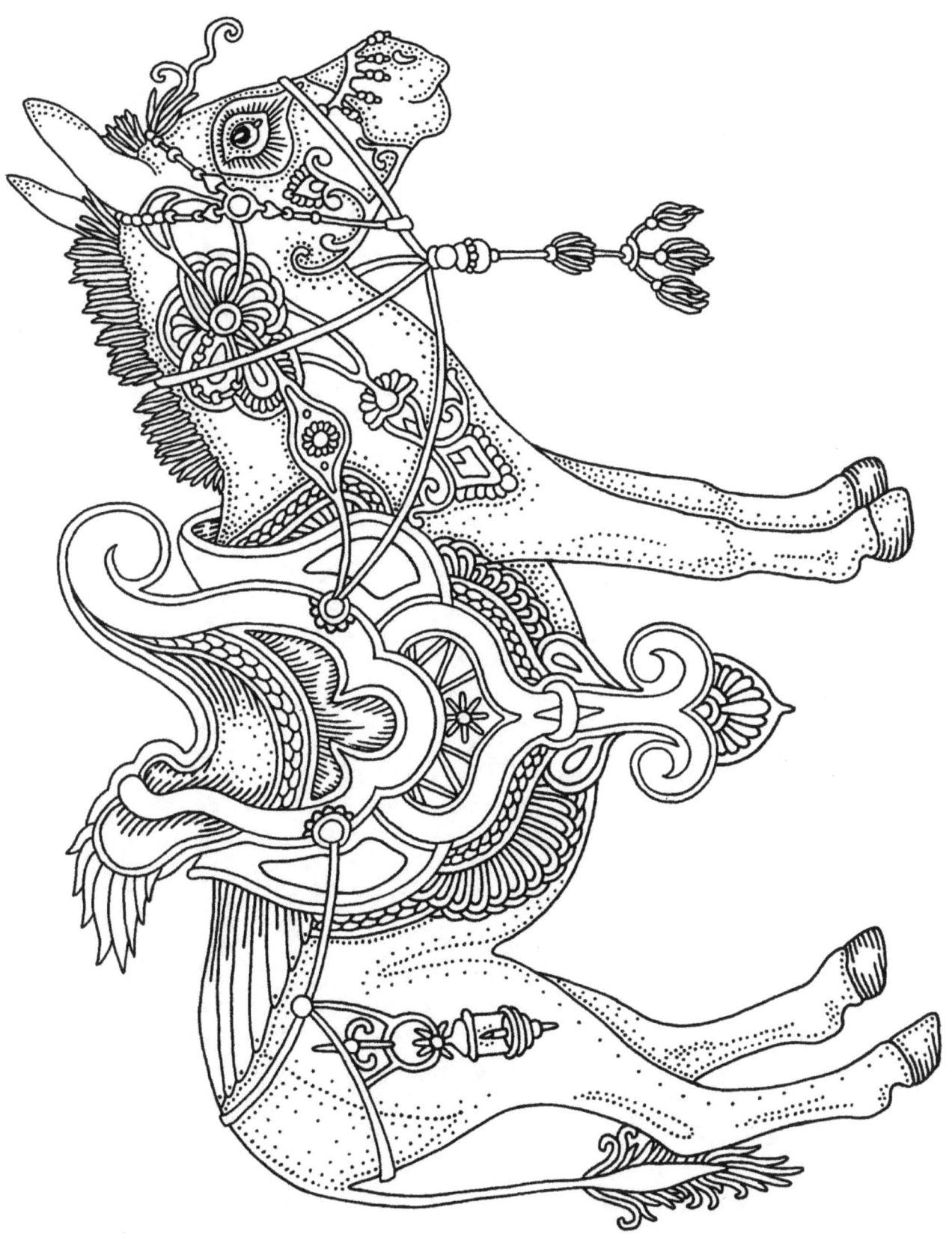

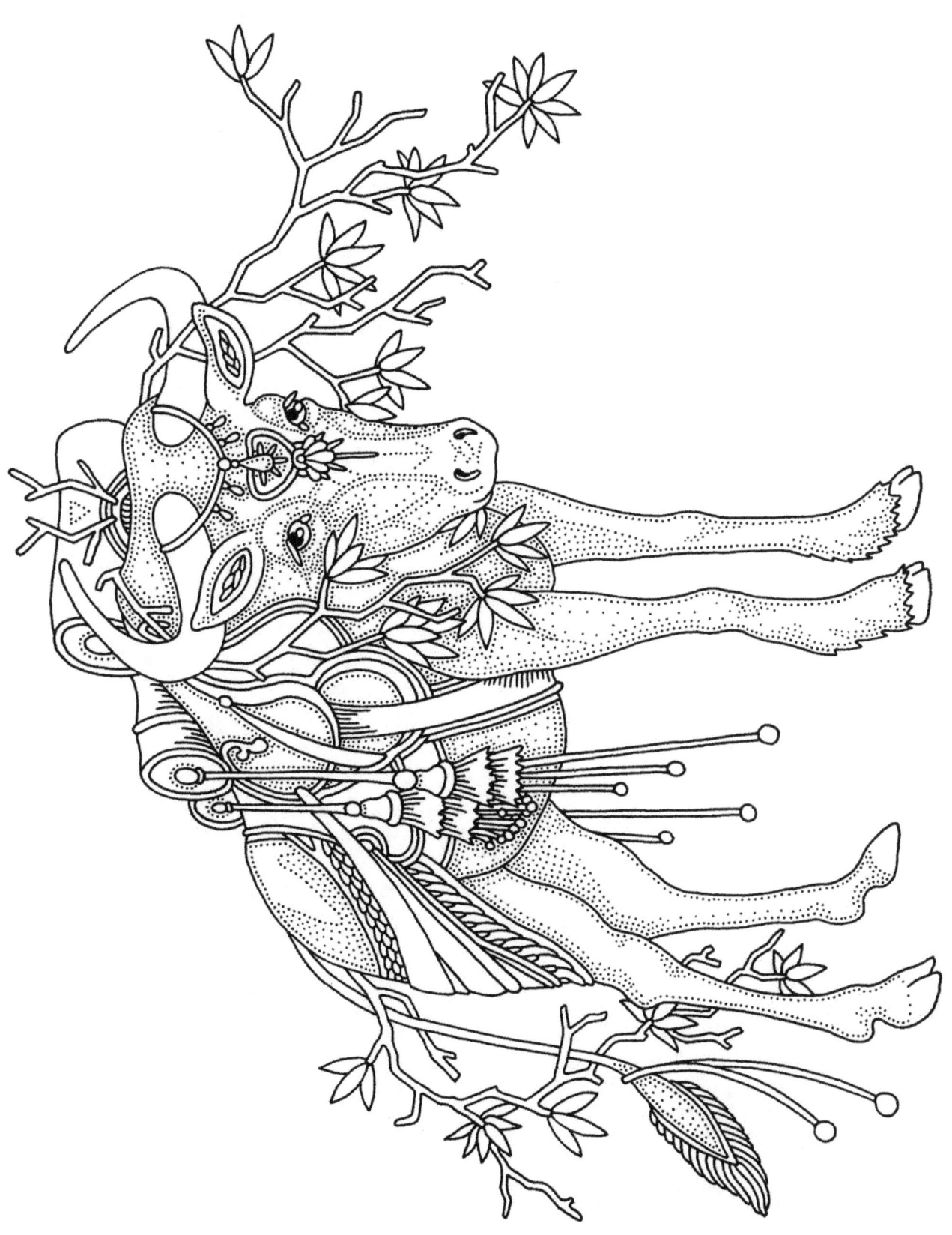

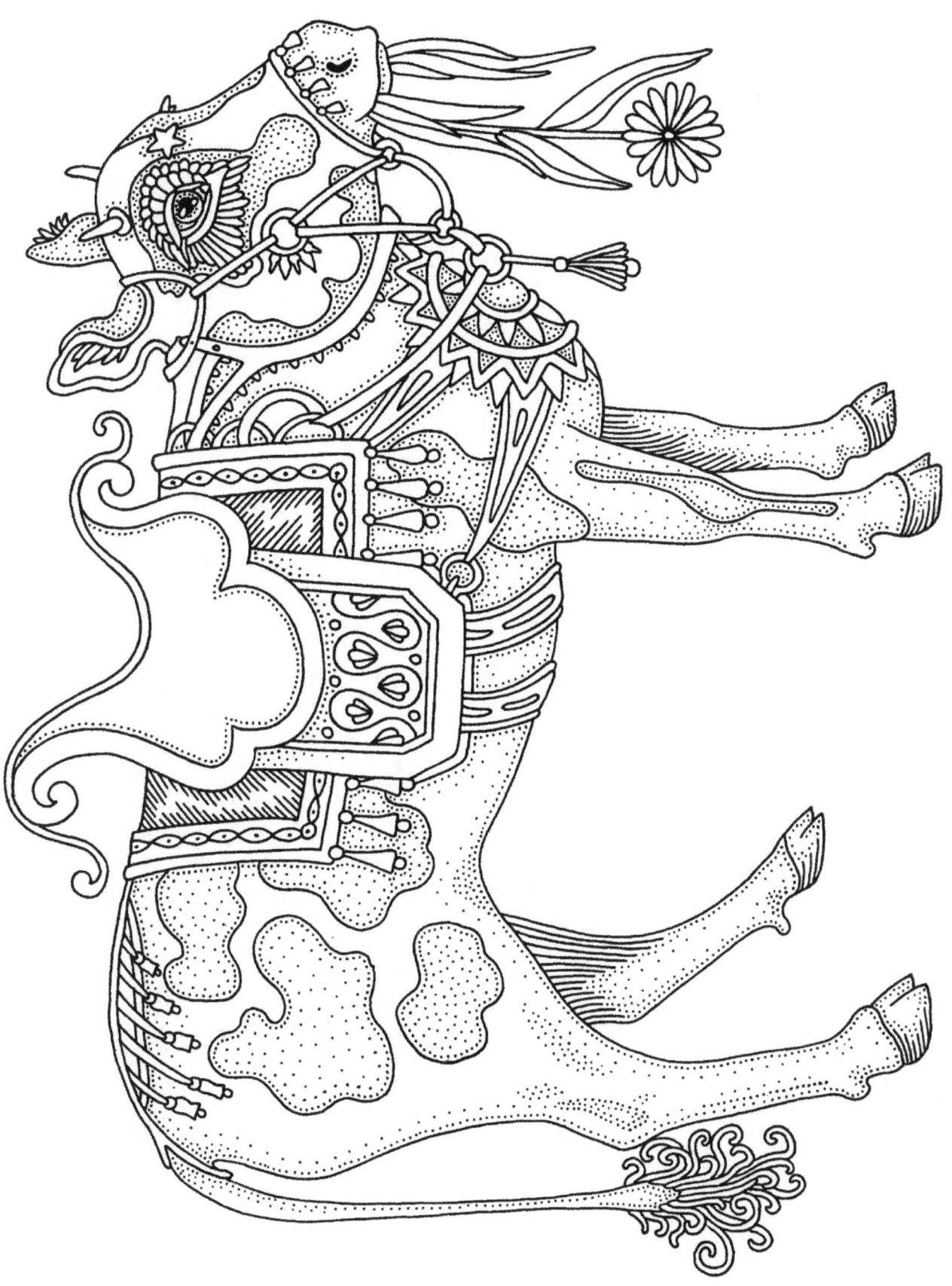

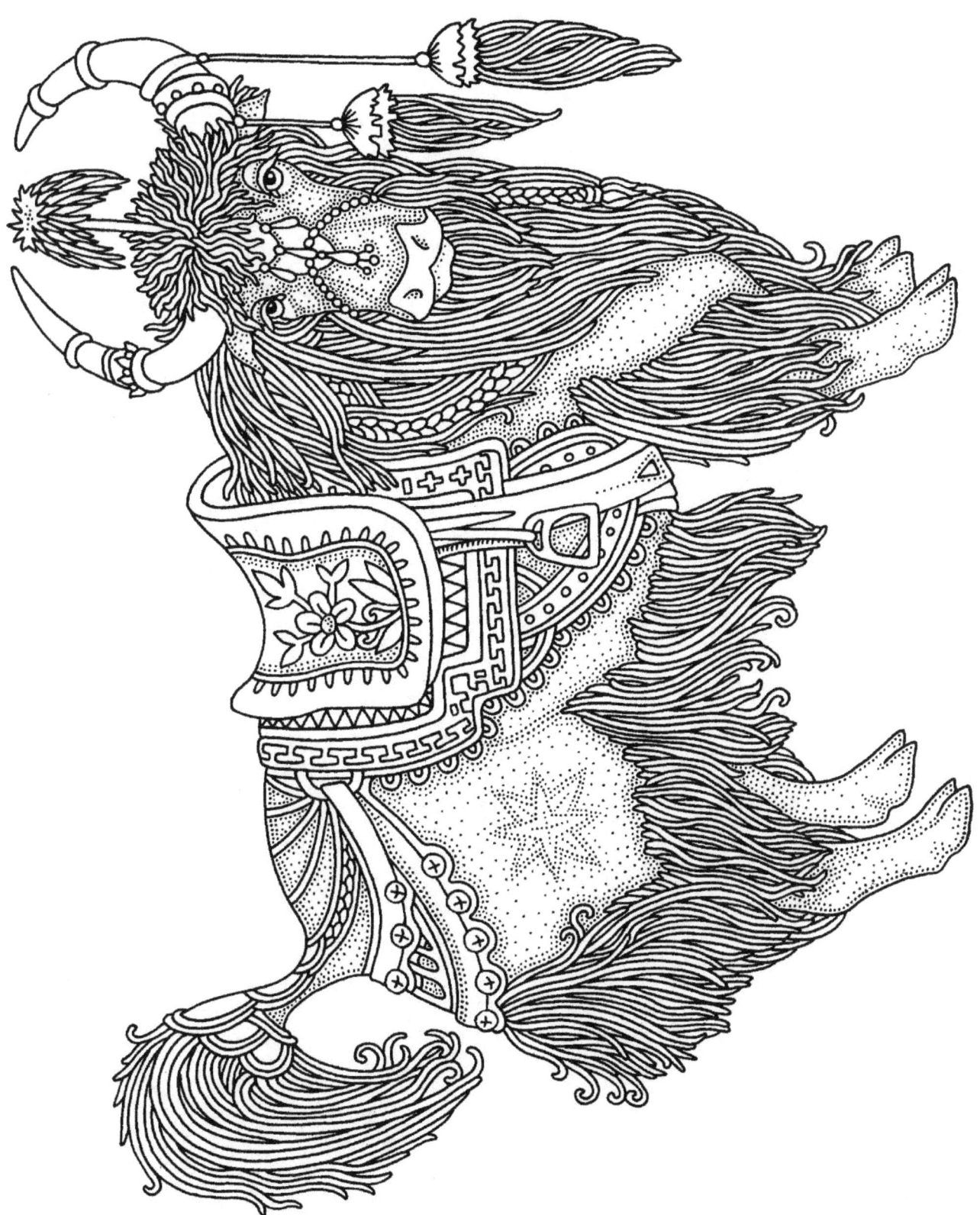

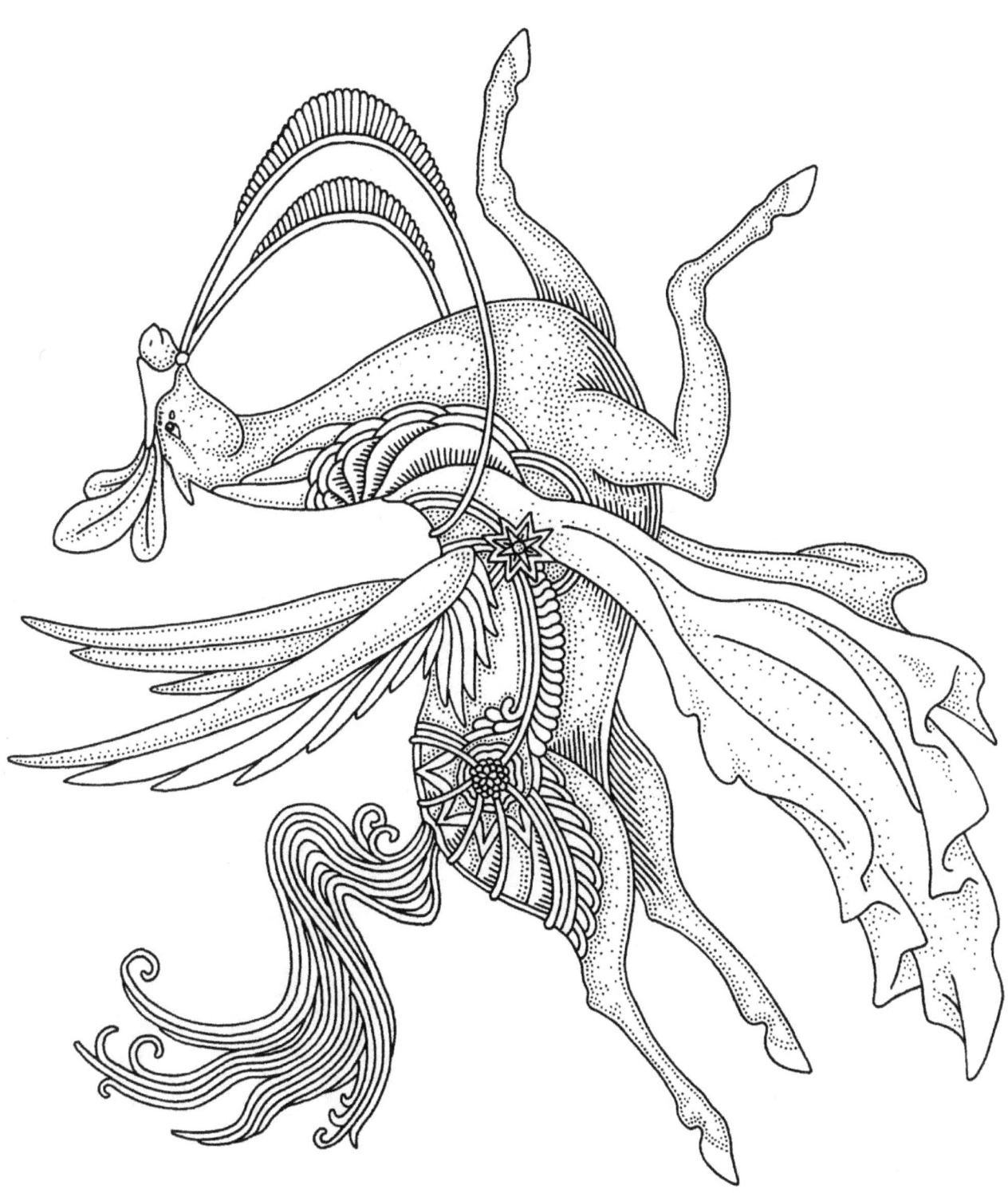

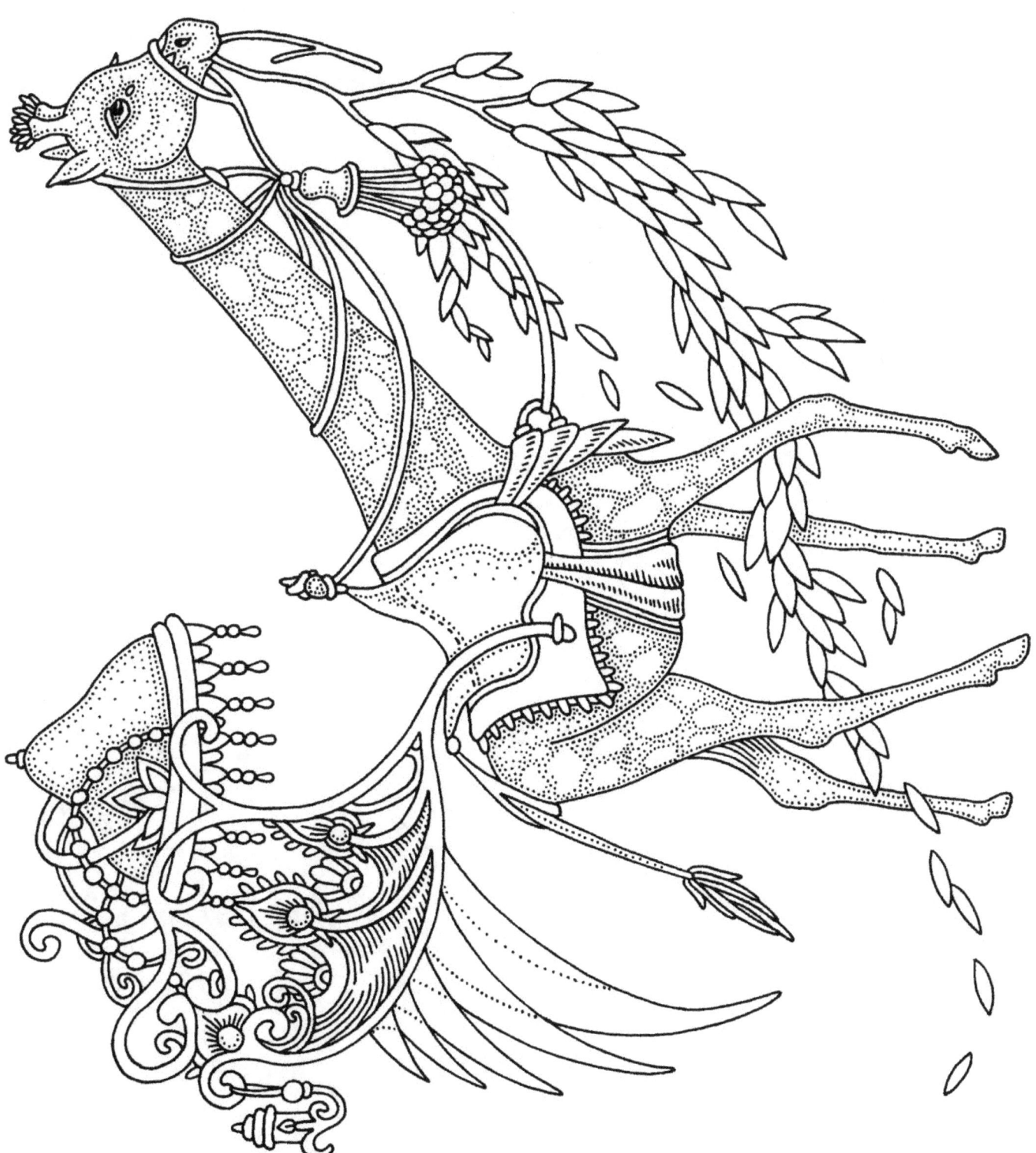

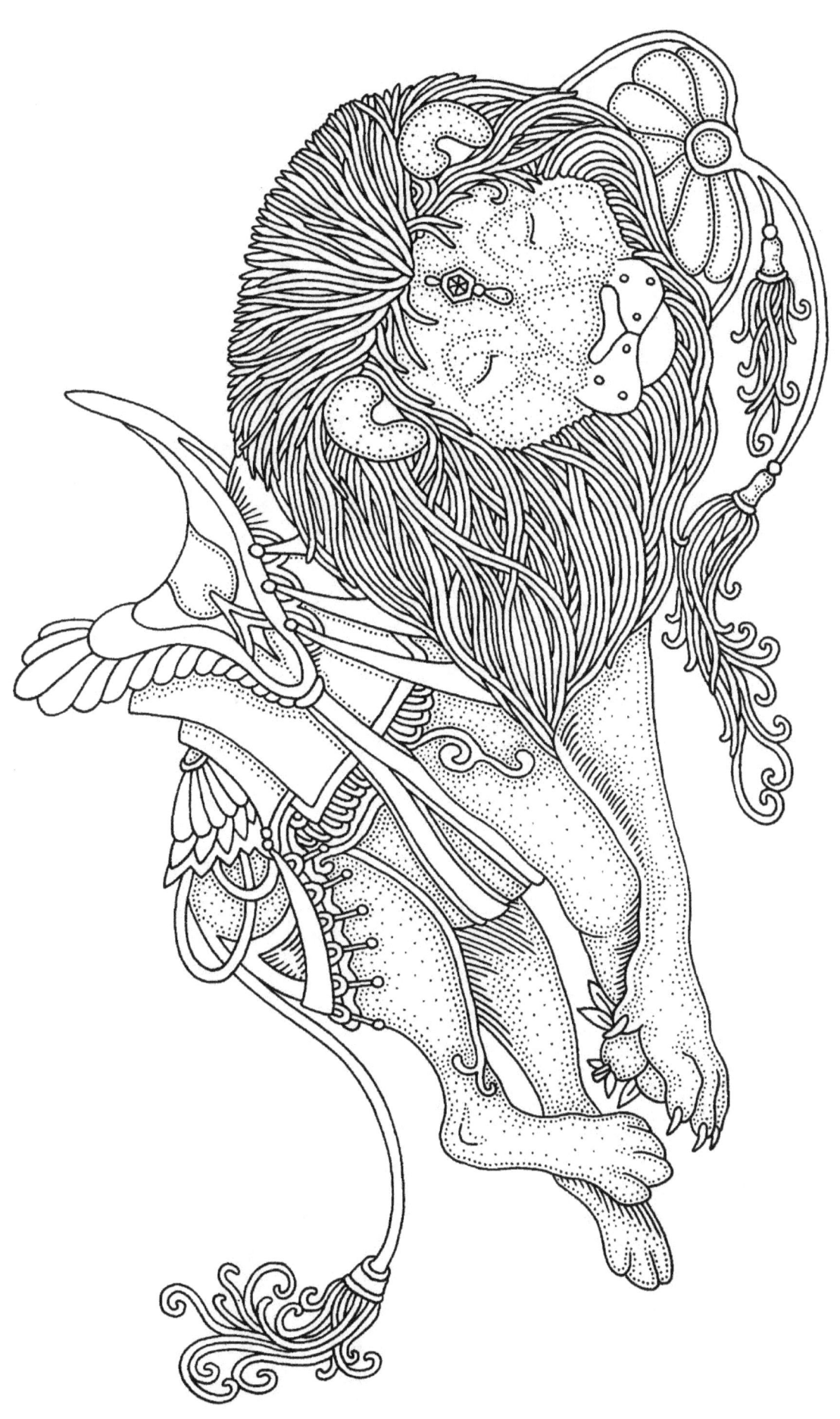

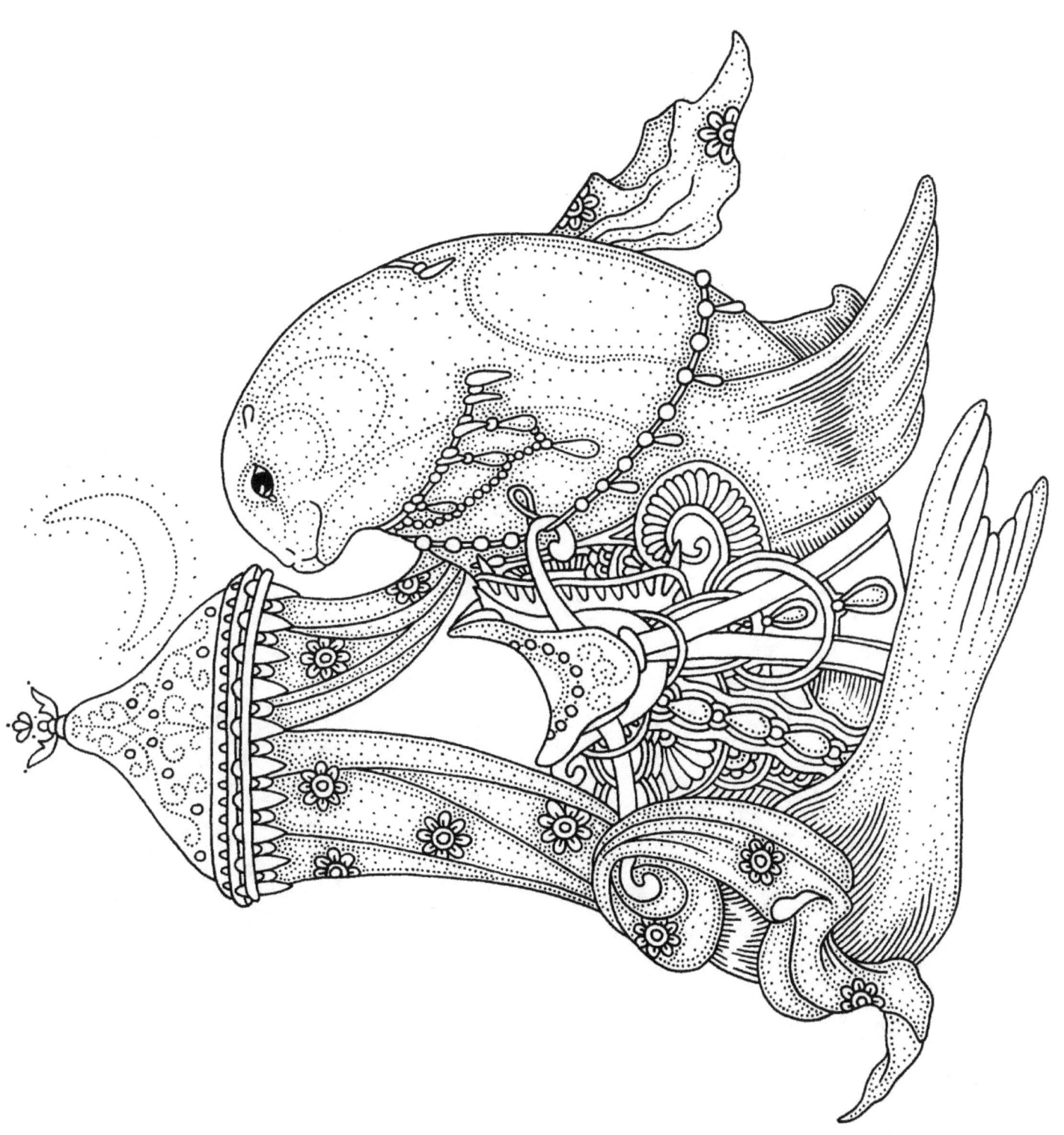

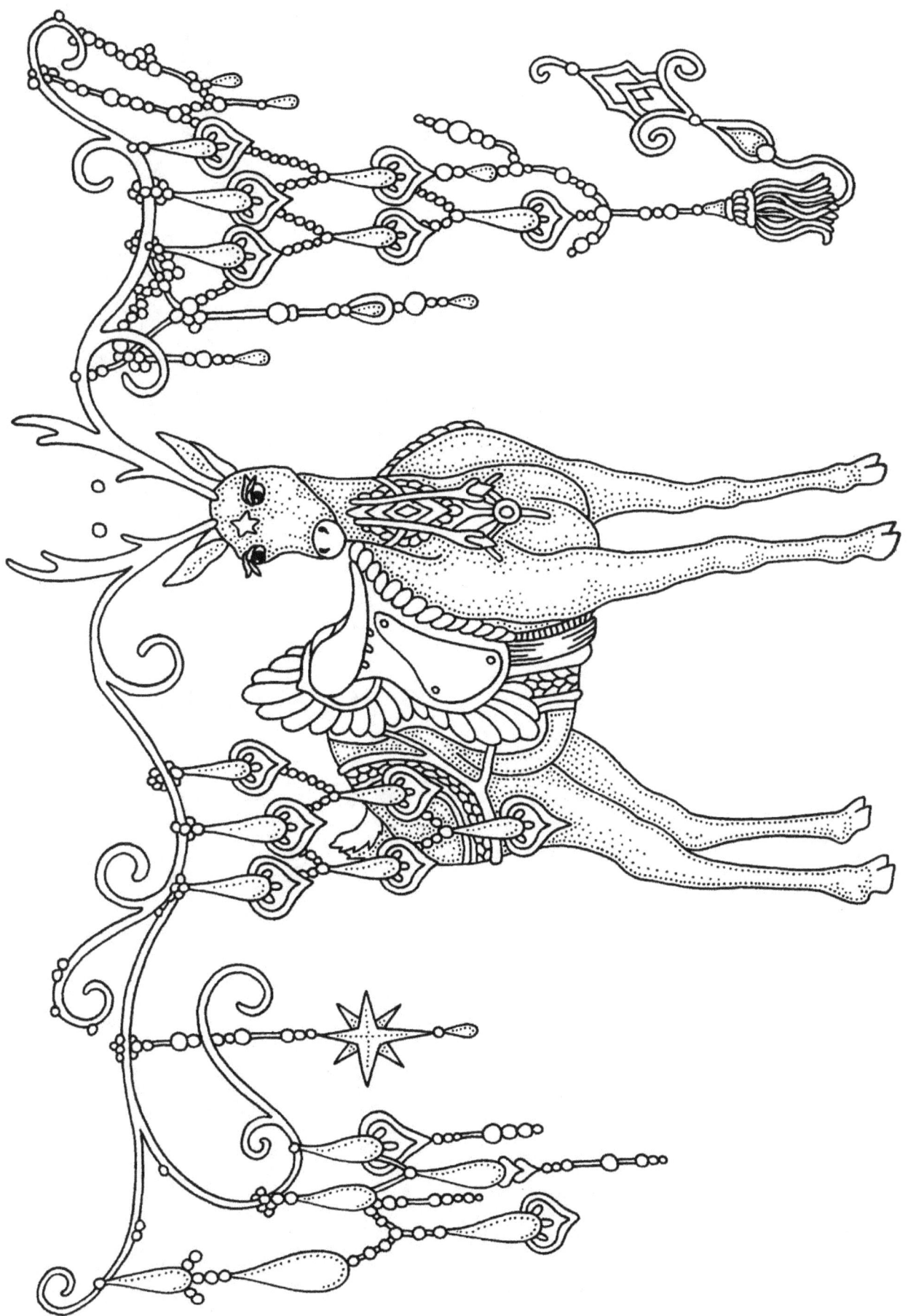

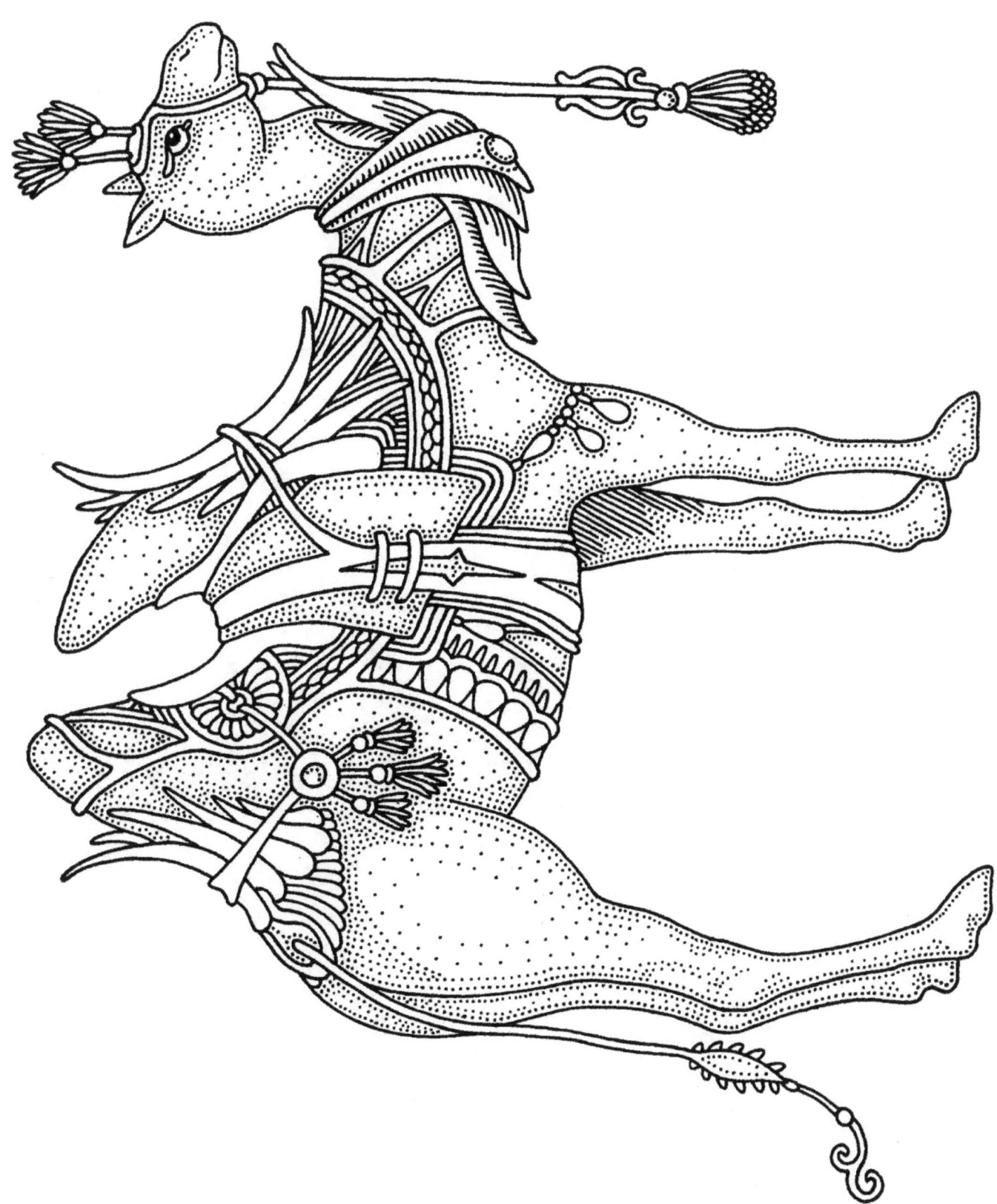

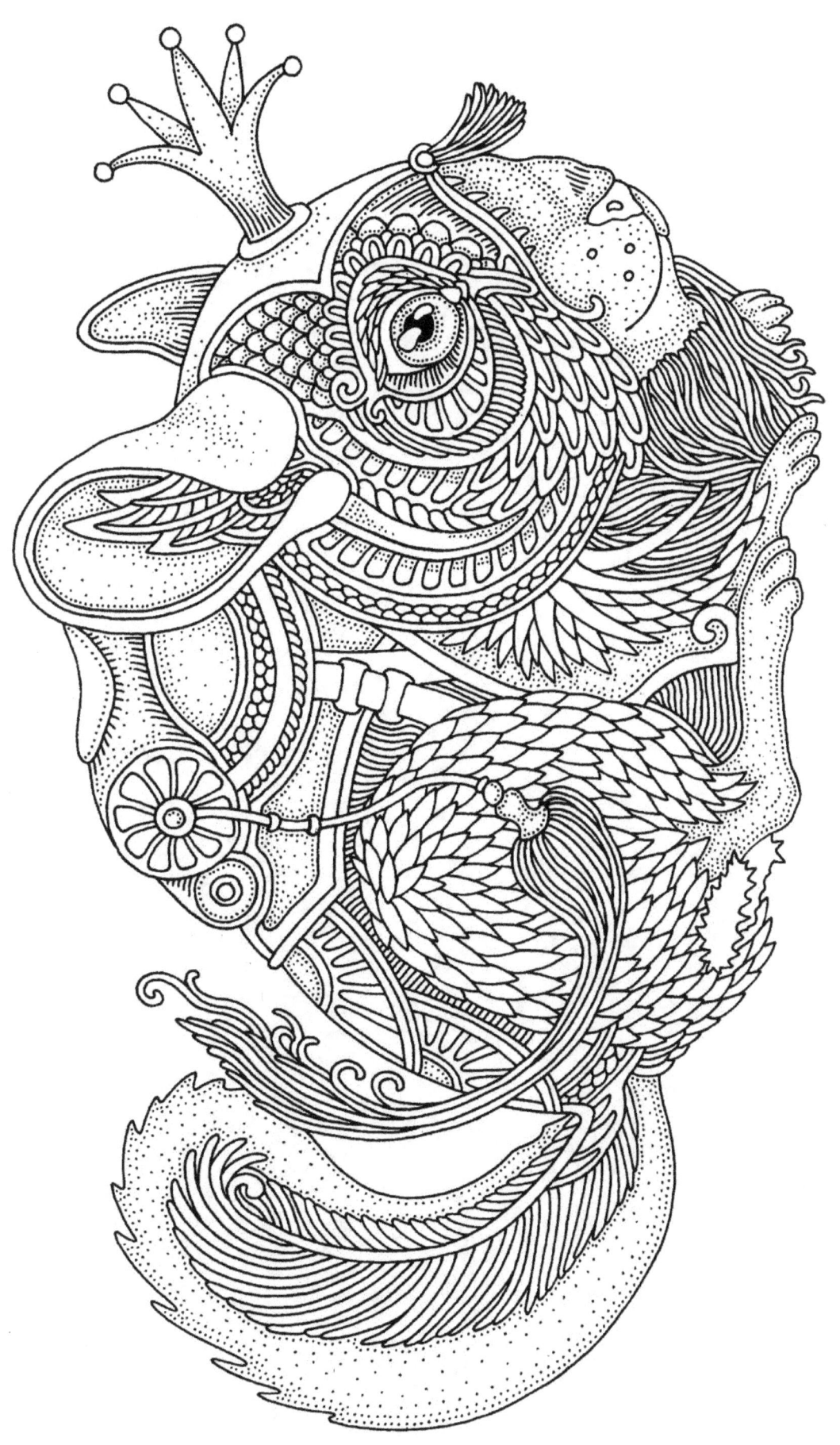

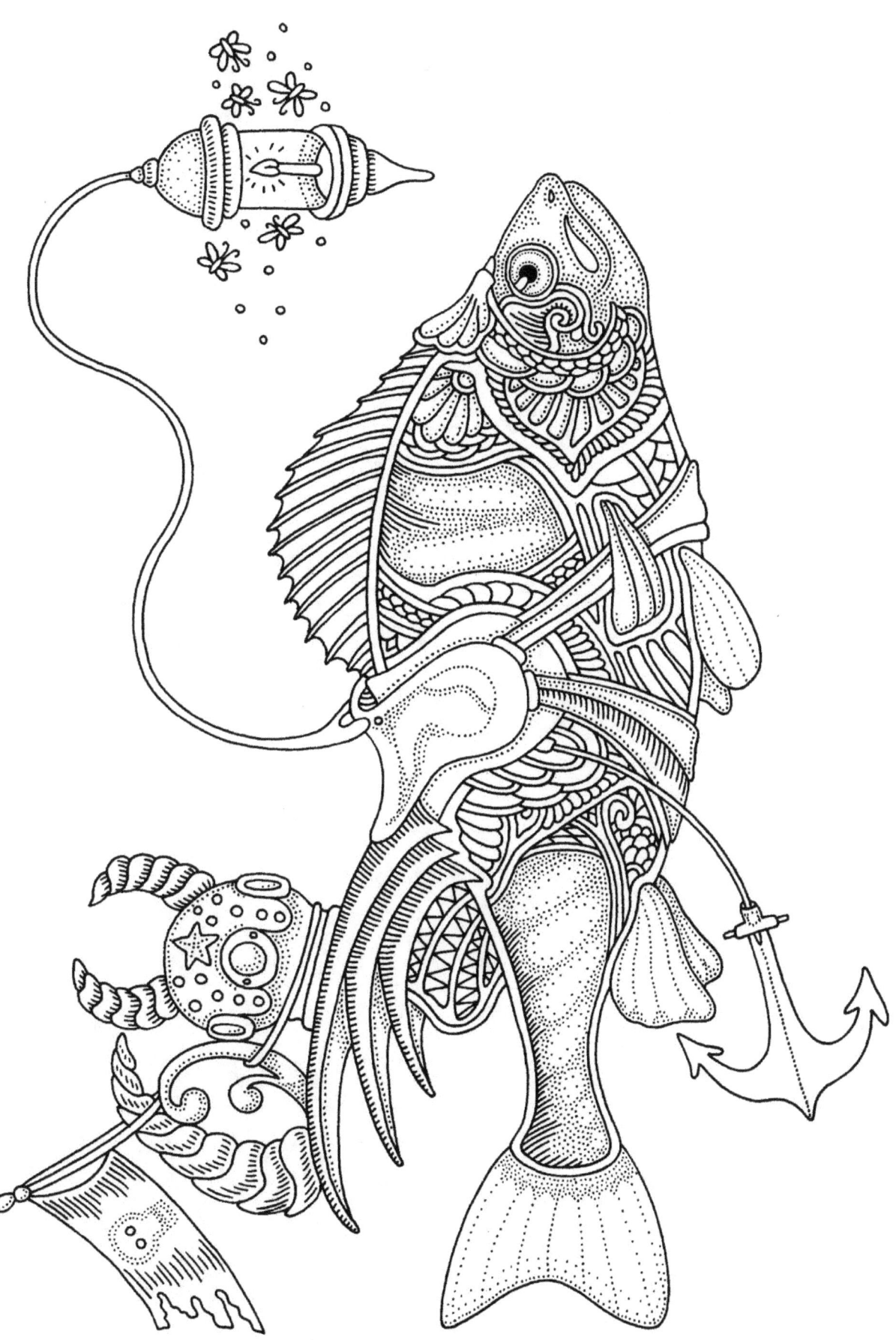

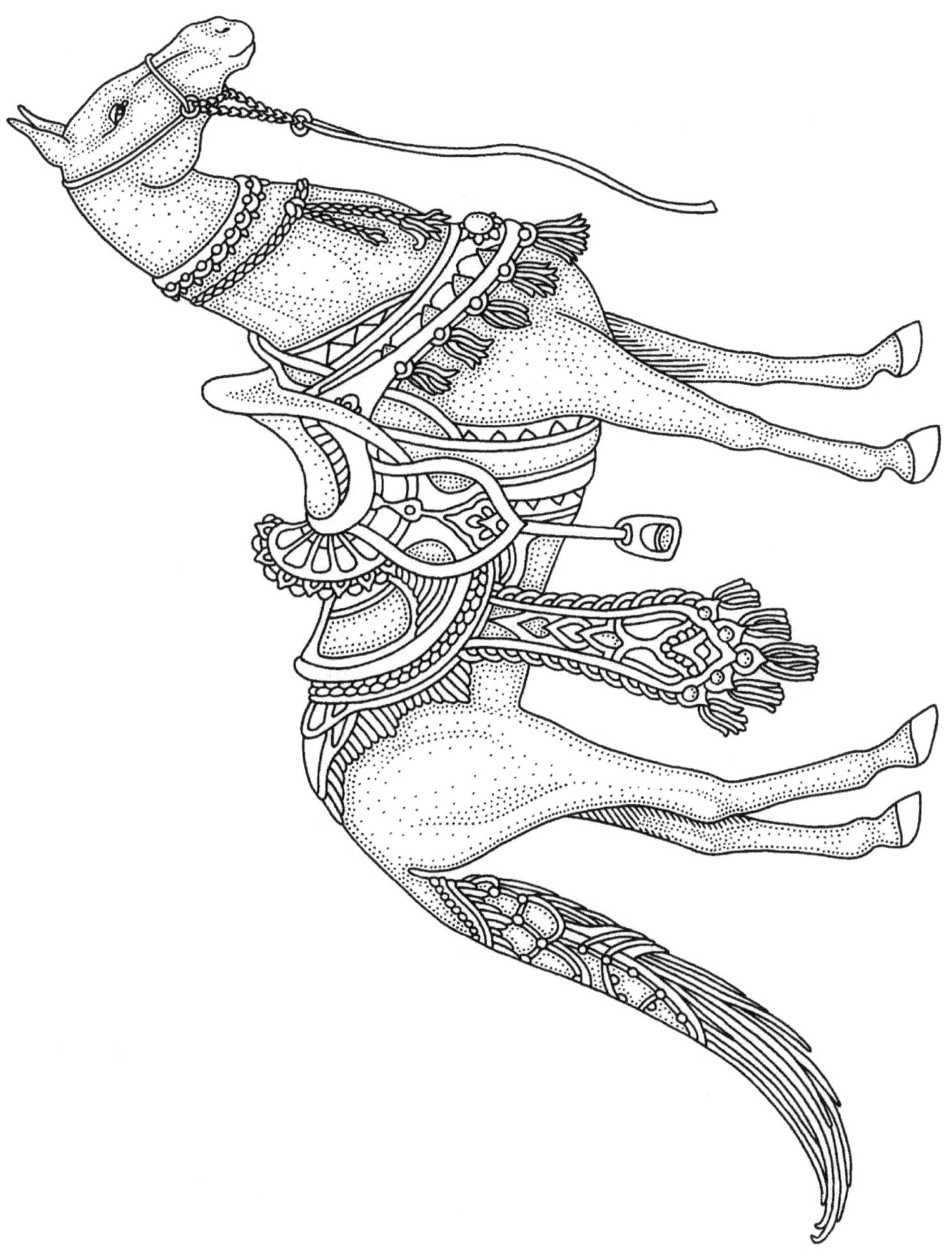

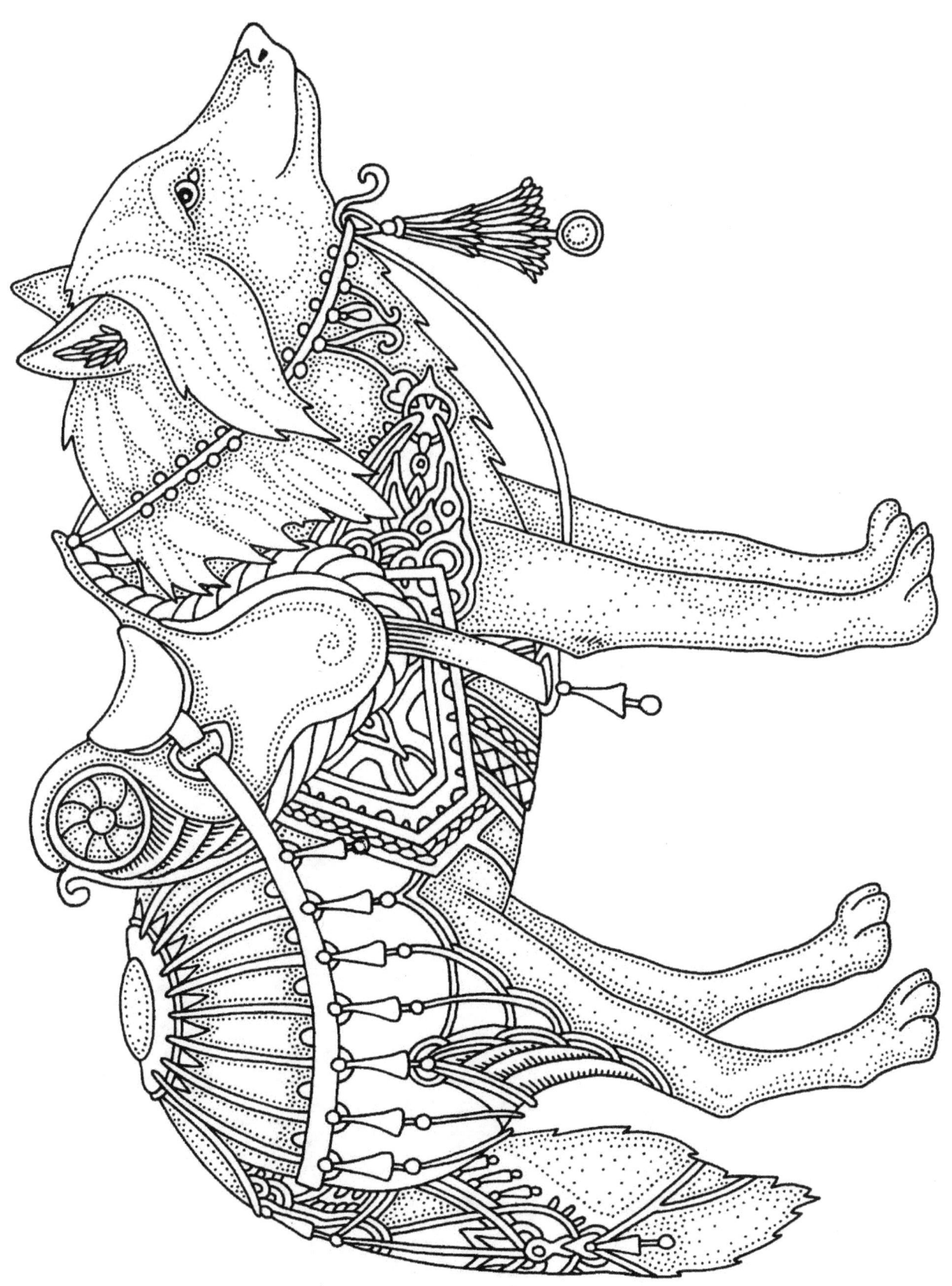

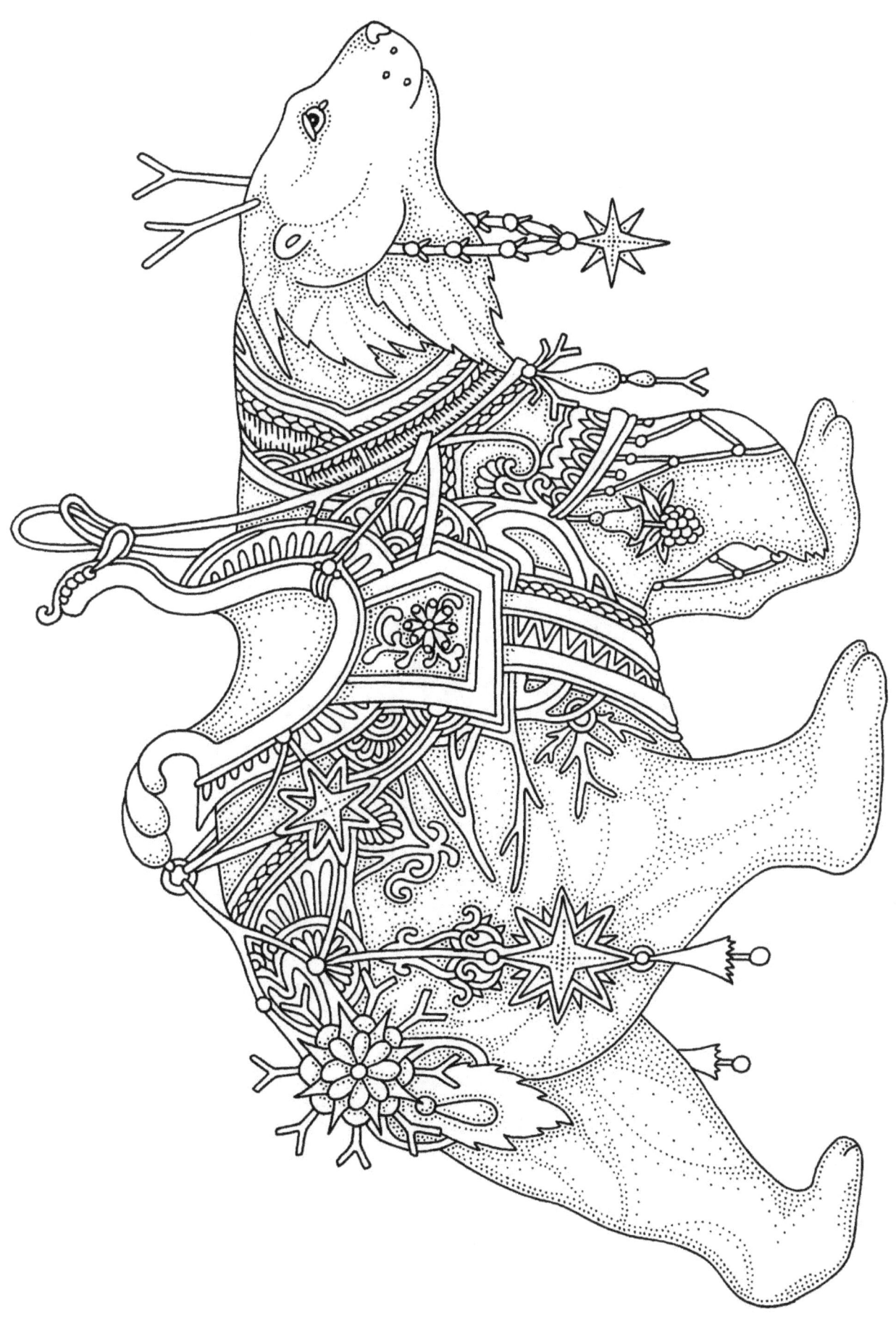

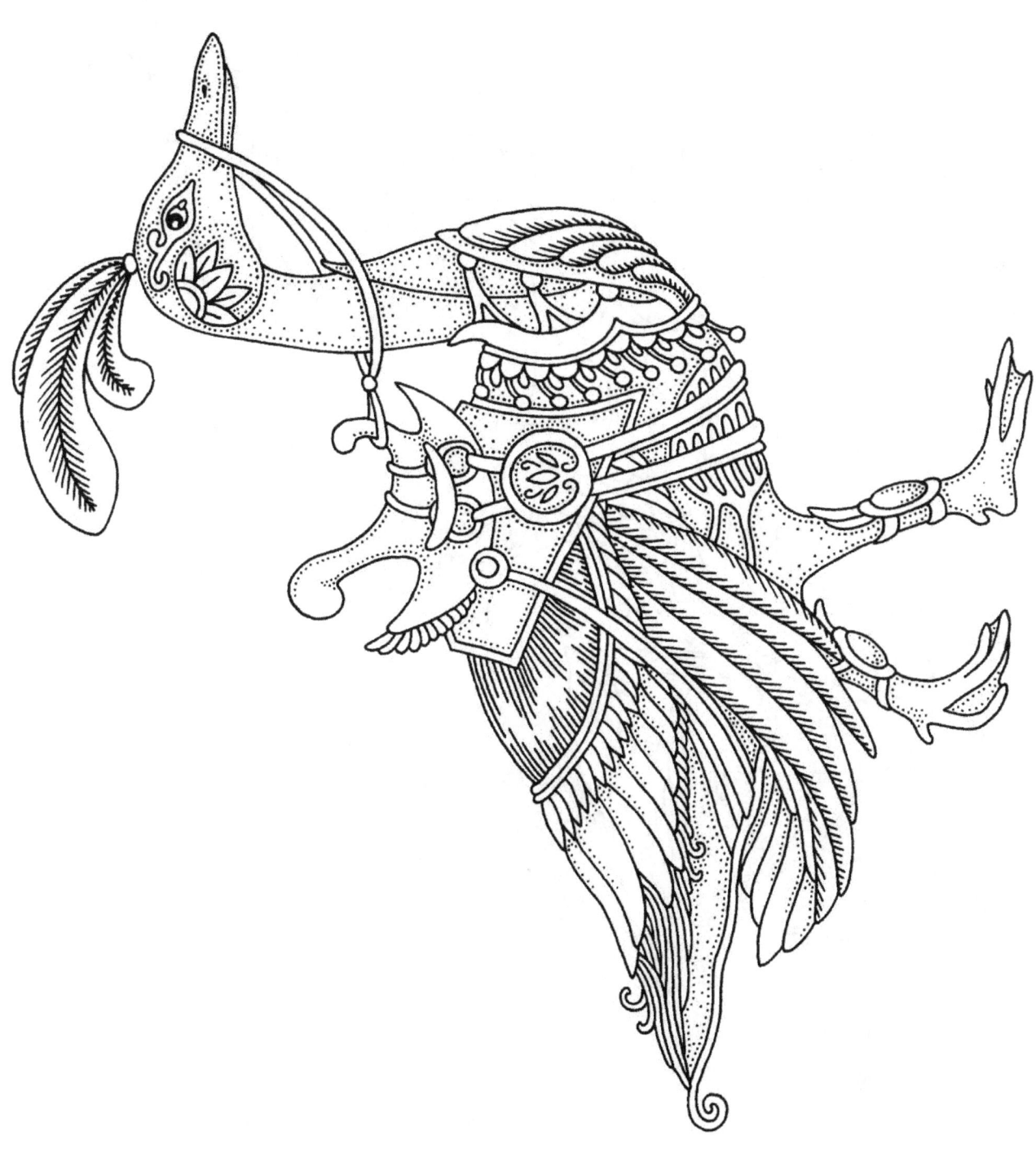

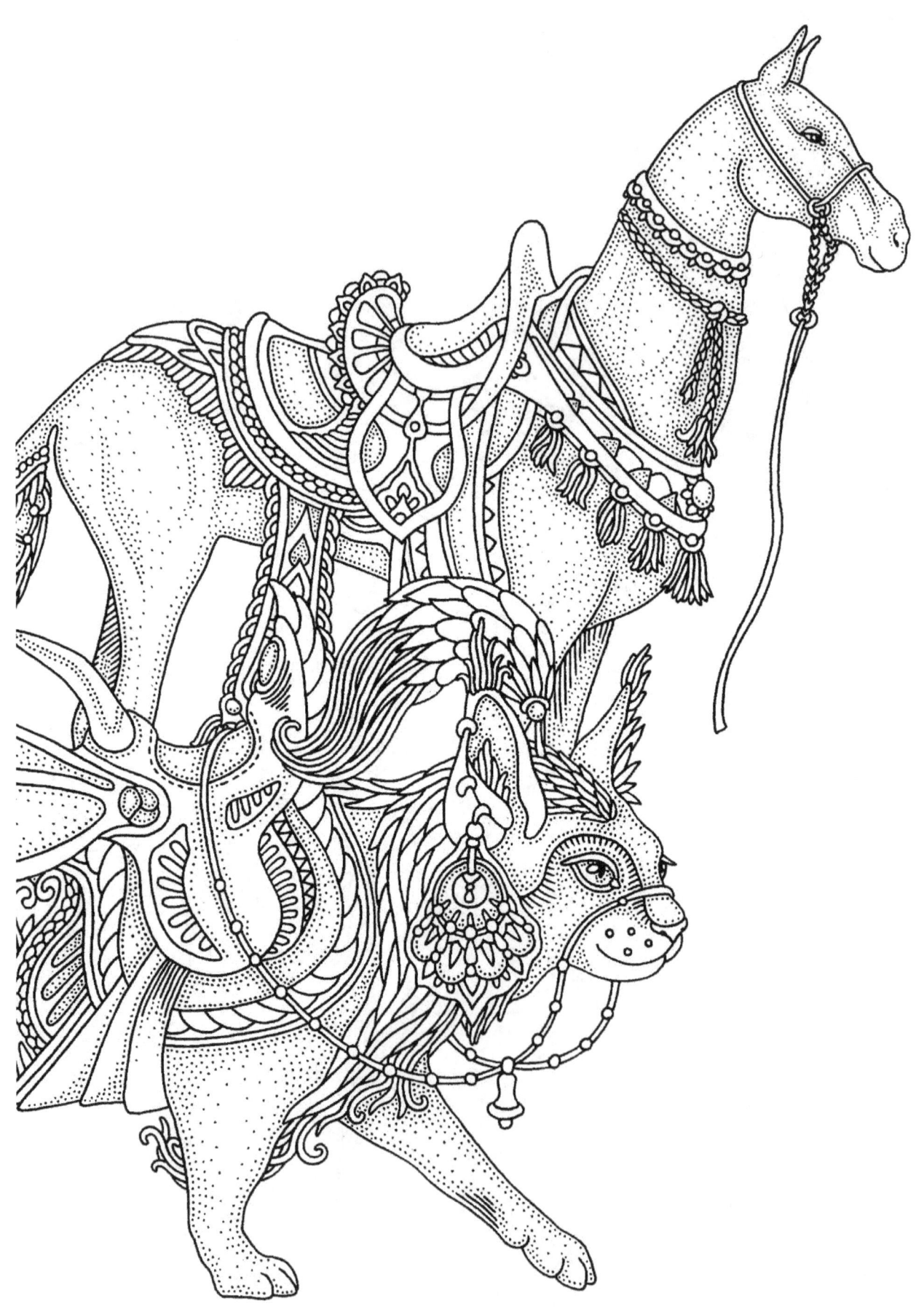

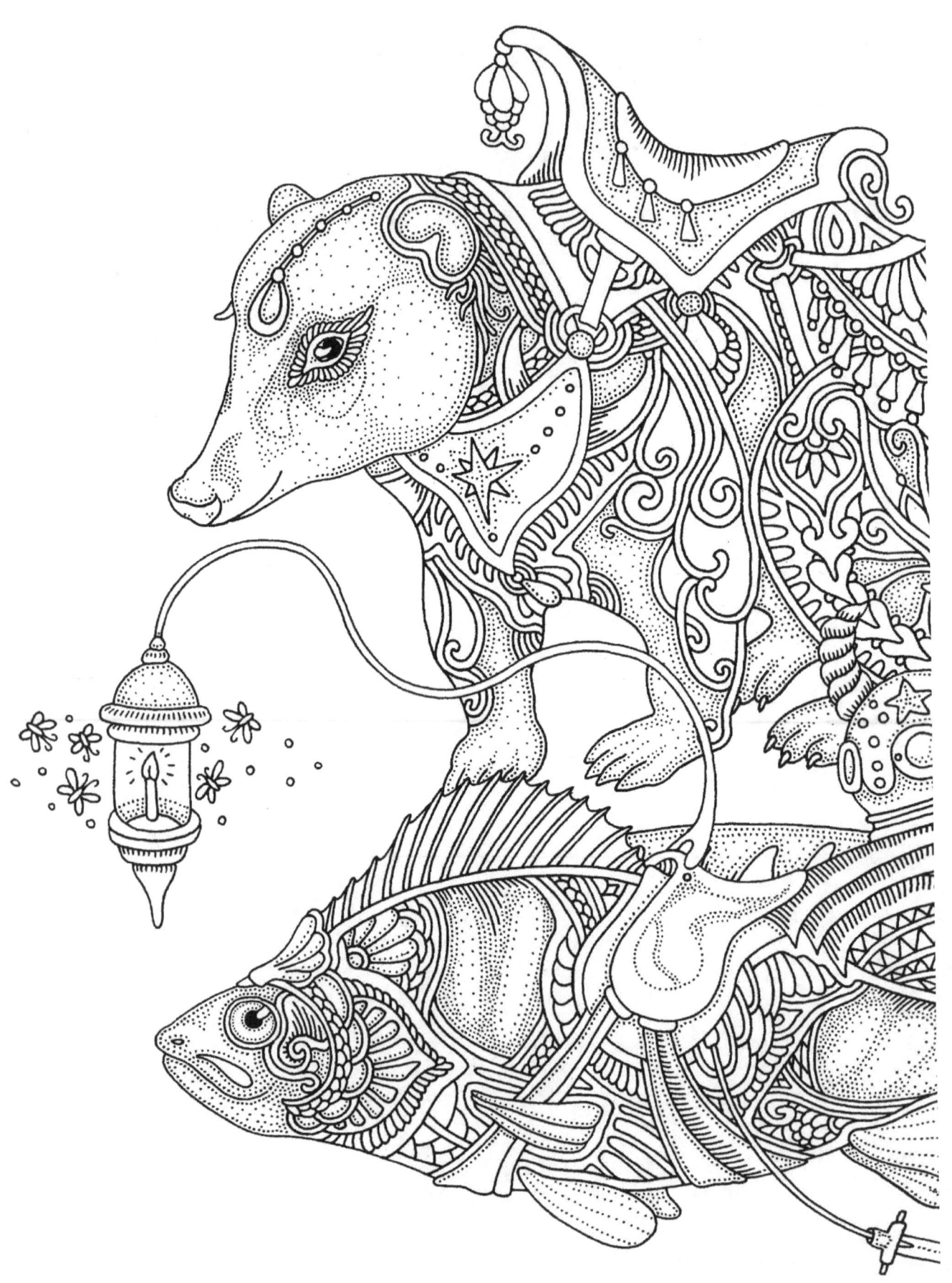